IT'S ALL GOOD... EXCEPT WHEN IT'S NOT (AND HOW TO KEEP GOING ANYWAY)

PRACTICAL MINDSET TOOLS FOR NAVIGATING LIFE'S CHALLENGES

NARELLE TODD

SUCCESSFUL
LIVING

To Ian Todd

Gone too soon. Missed deeply every day. It is a privilege to be your daughter.
"It's all good."

To my family — Dulcie, Cheryl and Stephen, Kevin and Mary

I struck gold in the family department. I love that we're friends and still have
each other's backs sixty years down the track. I love you.

To my dear friends — Caroline, Crystal, and Angela

I am blessed to call you friends. Thank you for always being there, even when
I didn't know I needed you.

To my family and friends in my Loving Lumpy Group

You were there for me every step of the way. I will never forget when, in a
particular dark period of radiation, I put out a call for funny memes and
jokes. You delivered like the legends you are and made my week brighter!

To Evey and Izzy

Your gift of Percy Parrot was perfect!

To every member of my medical team — seen and unseen

Thank you for your dedication to your profession. You saved my life, and I'm forever grateful. Any medical information I got wrong is on me, not you.

To my Get My Book Out There Mastermind group

Our weekly calls were a joy. I loved that, even though you were ready to go to battle for me to kick cancer's butt, you supported me by literally loving Lumpy to death.

To Nicola Bird and Gilly Woodhouse

My fierce business mastermind sisters — thank you for being my cheerleaders in opening my heart and pushing me to fully embrace my destiny.

To Caitlin McCoskey

Your energy work made all the difference. Thank you.

To Susan Smith aka S.E. Smith

Keep sparkling — the world needs your magic! Thank you for believing in me when I could not yet see it for myself.

And to anyone navigating their own challenges

This book is for you. May you find the courage, resilience, and humor to remind yourself... It's all good.

It's All Good… Except When It's Not (and How to Keep Going Anyway)

Practical Mindset Tools for Navigating Life's Challenges

© 2025 by Narelle Todd

Published by Successful Living Pty Ltd

https://www.narelletodd.com/

ISBN: 978-1-7638683-4-2 (Paperback)

ISBN: 978-1-7638683-0-4 (eBook)

Cover Design by 100 Covers, https://100covers.com/

Edited by S.E. Smith, https://sesmithfl.com/

* * *

* * *

This book is intended for informational purposes only and is the result of the author's personal experiences and beliefs. The author of this book is not a licensed medical professional, and the contents herein should not be considered medical advice.

The practices and approaches discussed in the book are not a substitute for professional medical advice, diagnosis, or treatment. Always seek the advice of your doctor or other qualified healthcare provider with any questions you may have regarding medical condition or treatment and before undertaking a new health care regimen. Never disregard professional medical advice or delay in seeking it because of something you have read in this book.

The author and publisher of this book disclaim any liability arising directly or indirectly from the use of the material provided in this book.

DESCRIPTION

What if your greatest challenge revealed your deepest strength?

When life delivers the unexpected — like a cancer diagnosis or a personal crisis — it can feel like your world is crumbling under the weight of opinions, expectations, and fear. Everyone has advice: "Try this diet." "Meditate it away." "God will heal/help you if you're faithful." "Think positive, and it will all work out." But what if you could quiet those voices and focus on the one that truly matters — yours?

In *It's All Good... Except When It's Not (and How to Keep Going Anyway)*, Narelle Todd shares her raw, honest, and often hilarious journey through cancer, showing you how to take back control of your story. This is not about what others expect of you. It's about finding your own path, guided by your values and your trusted medical team, whoever that may be.

Narelle's practical wisdom, heartfelt reflections, and laugh-out-loud moments remind us that cancer — or any life challenge — doesn't define us. It's how we choose to live each day that matters.

This is not about surviving; it's about finding light in the darkest moments, uncovering joy in the ordinary, and creating a life you love — no matter what.

Perfect for anyone navigating a cancer diagnosis or facing life's curveballs, *It's All Good... Except When It's Not (and How to Keep Going Anyway)* will help you:

• Quiet the noise of other people's expectations.

• Reclaim your voice and trust your instincts.

• Tap into your inner resilience, courage, and humor.

Discover how to live life on your terms, face the unexpected with grace, and find moments of joy — even on the hardest days.

CONTENTS

Introduction   xi

1. Background to Loving Lumpy   1
2. It's All Good — Lessons from My Dad's Cancer Journey   11
3. Project Loving Lumpy — Reframing Cancer with
   Humor and Love   17
4. Facts About Parotid — Facing the Unknown   26
5. Firsts   32
6. Operation Dumping Lumpy - Preparing for Surgery
   with Intention and Resilience   36
7. And I'm Back — Minus Lumpy!   44
8. How Loving Lumpy Flicked the Switch for Me —
   Finding Clarity and Taking Control   48
9. Storytelling — How Sharing My Journey Changed
   Everything   57
10. Update March 15th – 1st Visit Since Surgery   64
11. How Did I Get To Be So Calm? — Finding Balance in
    the Chaos   72
12. Celebrating With The Chickens — Finding Joy in
    Unexpected Places   82
13. The Reality of the Possible Complications Hit Me   88
14. March 27th — Finding Comfort in Connections   92
15. How Do I Look So Good After Surgery   94
16. Post Surgery #2   98
17. Update March 29th   102
18. Update March 30th   105
19. Update March 31st   108
20. Update April 1st   111
21. Update April 11th - Clear Lymph Nodes and a Future
    Bell Ringing!   114
22. Update April 18th — The Mask, the Plan, and a
    Tantrum in the Making   119
23. Update May 8th — Start of Radiation with Percy Parrot
    by My Side   124
24. Update May 10th   130
25. Update May 12th   132

26. Week 1 Radiation Wrap-up — The Highs, the Lows, and Percy Parrot   134

27. Update May 16th   138

28. How to Help a Low-Maintenance Friend   140

29. Support Network   146

30. Update May 22nd Week 3   151

31. Most Chilled Patient   156

32. Radiation Plan   157

33. No Taste Buds   161

34. Update May 29th — Staying in the Step You're In   163

35. Update June 2nd- Snot Happens   170

36. Update June 3rd — When Life Tastes Like Tin   174

37. Update June 4th   177

38. Update June 5th—The Power of One Small Fix   179

39. Update June 12th- Embracing the Boring Moments   182

40. Update June 14th- All Clear and Good to Go!   186

41. Update June 16th - Free at Last!   190

42. Update June 20th   195

43. Update July 31st   199

44. Update August 2nd-Blood Clot Update   203

45. Moving Forward — The Journey Continues   207

A Note from the Author   211

Tools to Light the Way   215

About the Author   219

INTRODUCTION

I fell in love with words and their power early on in life and they have always been my grounding source. When I was diagnosed with cancer, I did what I've always done when life gets challenging — I turned to words. I wrote regular updates, sharing my experiences, my thoughts, and, quite often, my humor, with my family and friends through a private Facebook group. Those posts became a way for me to process what I was going through and, at the same time, stay connected with the people I love.

This book is a collection of those posts, shared exactly as they were written at the time — raw, real, and sometimes a little irreverent (because laughter, let me tell you, is a superpower). But now, with the benefit of time, I've gone back and reflected on those updates. I've pulled out the lessons and insights I've gained along the way, and I've paired them with practical exercises to help you strengthen your own resiliency muscle.

My wish for you is that these reflections and takeaways help make the road a little easier. Whether you're navigating your own health journey, supporting someone you love, or simply trying to make sense of life's curveballs, I hope this book offers you comfort, perspective, and maybe even a chuckle or two.

We all face challenges in life. My journey has taught me that resilience isn't about pushing through without feeling — it's about acknowledging the hard parts and finding ways to move forward with grace, strength, and a little bit of humor.

Your strength runs deeper than you know, your courage shines brighter than you think, and your resilience grows with every step forward.

* * *

If you're ready to dive deeper into building your resilience and cultivating a powerful mindset, I've created a companion **Workbook** to guide you every step of the way. This step-by-step resource is designed to help you step into your strength, shed your fears, and embrace your journey with confidence. Find it here: https://itsallgo odbook.com/workbookitsallgood

* * *

Think of this as your sidekick for the journey ahead.

Because even when life gets tricky, you've got this... and a little extra support never hurts.

BACKGROUND TO LOVING LUMPY

I believe it's always helpful to know who the writer is at the start of a story like mine. Understanding where a person starts — their beliefs, experiences, and strengths — helps you appreciate the transformation they go through when life turns upside down. So, let me give you a little background about me, my experiences with cancer, and what my belief system looked like before my diagnosis.

My Family's History with Cancer

My first close encounter with cancer was through my grandmother and father, both of whom had melanomas. My grandmother survived three different melanomas and the invasive surgeries of the 1980s. Thankfully, neither my Dad nor Gran passed away from their melanomas. Gran lived well into her 90s, but my Dad's story was different, although it was not melanoma related cancer that impacted him.

Dad was diagnosed with glioblastoma, a fast-growing and highly aggressive brain tumor, in 2000, and passed away just over a year later. Dad's illness brought home to me in a very personal way that not every cancer story ends with a cure. No amount of treatment, prayer, or mindset work would change the outcome in his case. Sometimes, cancer wins.

In 2018, my sister Cheryl, whom I'm very close to, was diagnosed with breast cancer. Her year of chemotherapy, surgery, and radiation was brutal, but she made it through. Now, seven years later, she's cancer-free, and living a wonderful life.

These experiences taught me an important lesson: there's no guaranteed storybook ending with cancer (or any challenge). When my own diagnosis came, my immediate thought was, "No one knows how this will play out. The only thing I can control is how I live each day."

Lessons from Dad and Cheryl

The year my dad battled brain cancer was emotionally overwhelming. He stayed with me for a long period during his treatment, and the constant emotional swings became exhausting. I realized that riding those emotional waves wasn't healthy for anyone.

When Cheryl was diagnosed, we approached her cancer differently. We talked about what we had learned from Dad's experience and decided that humor would be our coping mechanism. We understood that any outcome was possible, and we chose to face it with laughter and love.

A Sprinkle of Woo-Woo

Before my diagnosis, I was someone who had invested in personal development with a light sprinkling of woo-woo. Let me clarify: I'm not hardcore woo. I'm not into past lives, reincarnation, soul contracts, or psychics. But I do believe in a higher power, in quantum physics, and that our minds are incredibly powerful tools.

I've always believed in creating a vision of life so strong that it consciously and unconsciously pulls you toward it. I also believe in writing things down to bring them to life — a lesson I learned from my "101 Things Before I Die" list.

The 101 List

Years ago, inspired by coffee table books like *101 Islands to Visit Before You Die*, I created my own list: *"101 Things I Want to Do Before I Die."* It included travel destinations like Iceland and Alaska, experiences like climbing the Sydney Harbour Bridge, and even meeting certain people, like Richard Branson and Julie Morgenstern.

Each year, instead of writing New Year's goals, I would pull out my list, check off what I had accomplished, and add new items to keep the list at 101 entries. There were no due dates or to-do lists, just a mix of achievable goals and "crazy impossible" dreams.

One such crazy dream was meeting Julie Morgenstern, a time management and organization guru. Years later, I sat next to her at a dinner, and we ended up chatting and recording an interview for my podcast. That moment taught me that the impossible can become possible without forcing it. I have also met Richard Branson, another person on my 101 List, but that is a story for another time.

Personal Development as My Foundation

My background in adult learning and development shaped my personal and professional life. I've always focused on helping people find calm through practical strategies, empowering them to live life on their terms.

I've explored various personal development models, from DISC and MBTI to Clifton Strengths and Human Design. These tools gave me valuable insights into who I am and what's important to me, which became a powerful foundation when I faced cancer.

If you haven't done personal development work before, don't worry — you don't need to rush off and complete every survey out there! Throughout this book, I'll share simple, practical questions to help you find clarity and live intentionally through any challenge. Think of this as your own personal and tailored personal development guide.

Living by Core Values

At the heart of everything I do are five core values:

1. Personal Accountability
2. Authenticity
3. Grace
4. Openness to Learning and Growth
5. Humor

I invite you to reflect on your own core values. When life throws challenges your way, these values can act as your anchor, helping you stay balanced and centered. By holding yourself steady in the storm, you'll find that emotional balance becomes easier to maintain.

If you are unsure how to work out your core values, I have a free guide for you here: https://www.narelletodd.com/identifymyvalues/

REFLECTIONS: WHO I WAS BEFORE CANCER

Before cancer entered my life, I thought I had a pretty good handle on things. I believed that what you focus on is what you see reflected back — look for the good, and you'll find it. I practiced that belief daily, seeking out the silver linings, just like my dad always did.

I loved to travel, because it opened me to new experiences and different ways of living. I'd wander through markets in foreign cities, marvel at centuries-old architecture, and immerse myself in the everyday lives of people around the world. Travel wasn't about ticking boxes on a bucket list; it was about seeing the world through fresh eyes and reminding myself that happiness isn't about what you own, but how you live your life.

The Life I Was Building

At that point in my life, my focus was clear: I was growing my business.

I'm a life and business coach, by both nature and training, and helping others achieve their dreams was what lit me up. I knew that by helping women find fulfillment in their work, that happiness would flow back into their homes, creating stronger families and healthier communities. I used to say, with a little twinkle in my eye, that I was on a mission to create world peace, one family at a time.

I was chasing a big financial goal of growing my business to $1 million in revenue, a number that had stuck with me since childhood. But by then, it wasn't just about hitting that number — it was about the impact I could have on others.

Nothing gave me more joy than helping people see new possibilities and lighting the path toward their dreams. Seeing a client's face light up when they realized a problem they thought was insurmountable had a solution?! That was everything to me.

The Fears I Faced

Despite my love of travel, I had a crippling fear of flying for years. I'd sit, white-knuckled, wide awake on flights, convinced the plane would crash if I let my guard down. It wasn't until I confronted the root of my fear — a need for control and a fear of death — that I could begin to relax. Once I let go of that illusion of control, flying became a joy instead of a terror.

Interestingly, I never feared serious illness, particularly cancer. I went to my regular mammograms and cervical checks, but the thought of being diagnosed with cancer felt like a distant, almost impossible scenario. It just didn't seem like something that would ever happen to me.

My biggest health concerns at the time were maintaining healthy blood (due to Factor V Leiden*) and the total knee replacement (TKR) I knew I'd need to walk without pain. But cancer? Not on my radar.

Daily Practices and Mindset

I've always been someone who loves routine and personal growth practices. I dabbled in journaling, but my consistent practice has always been affirmations and meditations.

Every day at 7am and 3pm, affirmations pop up on my phone, and I stop whatever I'm doing to read them aloud three times, making sure I bring as much emotion to them as possible. These affirmations are fluid — I change them when needed or when I want to focus on something specific.

Looking back, those affirmations became an anchor for me once my world shifted with my cancer diagnosis.

The Quiet Doubts

Like many people, I've always had my share of self-doubts.

I knew I was good at what I did, but there were moments of imposter syndrome that crept in, whispering things like, "Who are you to think you can help people change their lives?"

I've never been one to share deeply personal things outside of my close-knit circle of friends. I was private by nature, choosing to keep my struggles to myself rather than open up to others.

But cancer has a way of changing your perspective. It strips away pretence and leaves you with raw truth. You can either bury yourself in that truth or share it to help others navigate their own difficult roads.

The Bigger Picture

At that time, my life was moving forward in a straight line. I had goals, routines, and a clear vision for my future. I knew where I was headed, and I felt in control of my destiny. Covid restrictions had ended and international travel was back on the cards. Friends and I were throwing around the idea of visiting Svalbard and Norway.

But we all know that control is an illusion.

Cancer taught me that life can change in an instant. It taught me that no one is promised tomorrow, and that the only day we truly have is the one we're living right now.

Looking back, I realize how unprepared-and prepared-I was to handle the news of my diagnosis. But I also realize that everything I was already doing — the affirmations, the personal growth work, my love for helping others — became my lifeline.

When It Was My Turn

When my cancer experience began, I knew I had to incorporate those past lessons. I asked myself key questions:

- "I am only here for this day. How do I want to live it?"
- "How do I want to experience my cancer?"
- "What do I want this journey to feel like?"

I had seen the extreme emotional highs and lows with my dad's cancer, and I knew I didn't want that for myself. With Cheryl's cancer, I took a more centered approach by educating myself on her disease and its treatments. Worry was still present, but it was tempered with the confidence that I could handle whatever came next because I had researched it. Plus, I was fully onboard with fighting breast cancer.

When it came to my diagnosis, something surprising happened — one of the first thoughts that popped into my mind was, "I want to love my cancer."

It might sound strange, but it made perfect sense to me. My tumor was a part of me. I didn't want to fight it or go to war with myself.

Instead, I decided to love it. I was quite happy to love my cancer right out of my body, saying, "I love you, Lumpy, but you need to go!"

And that's how my year-long journey with "Loving Lumpy" began.

KEY TAKEAWAYS FOR YOU

I'd like you to consider these key lessons from my experience:

1. Your mindset is your greatest asset.

The way you think and talk to yourself matters more than you might realize. When you face a challenge, try to remember that it's your reaction that defines your experience.

2. You are more resilient than you think.

We all have a core of resilience inside us, but sometimes it takes a significant life event to uncover it. Trust that you can handle more than you think you can.

3. Live in the present.

I've learned that living in the moment brings peace. Worrying about the future or dwelling on the past only robs us of today's beauty.

A PRACTICAL TAKEAWAY FOR YOU

Before my cancer diagnosis, I believed that the way you see the world shapes what you experience. And I still believe that today. But there's something more I've learned — the importance of letting go of control and focusing on the present moment.

If you're going through a difficult time — or even if life is running smoothly right now — try this simple exercise to ground yourself in the present moment:

1. Take stock of what's working in your life right now.

It's easy to focus on what's going wrong, but it's just as important to recognize what's going right.

2. Pause and ask yourself: "What am I trying to control right now?"

Acknowledge that control is an illusion. The only thing we can control is our response to life.

3. Ask yourself: "How do I want to show up for this challenge?"

This question has been a game-changer for me. It puts me back in control and reminds me that my response is my choice.

4. Choose one thing you can do today to bring joy or ease.

Whether it's reading affirmations, taking a walk, or savoring a cup of coffee, be present in that moment.

5. Repeat this mantra:

"It's all good."

It's a simple phrase, but it's one that reminds me of my dad's wisdom. No matter what life throws your way, there is always something to be grateful for, something to find joy in.

That's what I've learned from reflecting on where I started before my cancer diagnosis.

What I Didn't See Coming

At that point in my life, I thought I was on track. I thought my biggest challenges were growing my business and getting a new knee.

I never expected that my life would soon be turned upside down by Lumpy — my cancerous tumor.

But if there's one thing I've learned, it's that you don't need to be ready for everything life throws at you.

You just need to trust that you'll find a way through.

* * *

*Factor V Leiden is a genetic mutation of one of the blood's clotting factors that increases the risk of developing abnormal blood clots, particularly in the legs or lungs.

IT'S ALL GOOD — LESSONS FROM MY DAD'S CANCER JOURNEY

When my dad was diagnosed with glioblastoma brain cancer in December 1999, my world shattered.

I was living in leafy Sydney, painting the walls of my new home, when I saw my dad and sister pull into the driveway after a doctor's appointment. I knew, even before they stepped out of the car, that something wasn't right.

Within hours, we went from shock diagnosis to major surgery scheduled two days before Christmas. It felt like life had slammed on the brakes and sent us all hurtling into a new, terrifying reality.

Navigating Grief and Fear

In those early months after Dad's diagnosis, I felt like I was living on a rollercoaster — swinging between hope, despair, anger, and sorrow.

Dad stayed with my sister and me for much of that year. Mum and Dad lived in the country and Dad's GP back home was very frank in saying that they weren't resourced to help him. We were renovating the house, I had a busy Human Resources Management job, so life was busy, and yet, beneath it all, there was this looming awareness that time was slipping away.

Dad was a farmer and had always been physically active — he couldn't just sit still. Even though the surgeon had warned him not to do heavy work, I'd come home to find him chopping wood for the fireplace. I remember going mad at him, frustrated that he wouldn't follow the doctor's advice. His response?

"I can't just sit around. I need to do something."

That was Dad. He was resilient, practical, and did not want to be a burden.

Watching Cancer Take His Voice

One of the hardest things to watch was cancer stealing Dad's ability to speak. The tumor was on the left side of his brain, affecting his speech and language.

Within three months, Dad found it difficult to speak, mixing his words. Within five months, Dad could no longer talk. My heart broke watching this man — who was incredibly articulate and loved to tell stories — lose the ability to communicate with his family.

It felt like the ultimate cruelty. Cancer had not only taken his health but also his voice.

I'll never forget the day Dad fell in the bathroom. He was so embarrassed that I had to help him up. He felt it wasn't right for me to see him like that — vulnerable, in pain. But in that moment, I felt nothing but love and heartbreak.

Finding Moments of Joy

Despite the relentless progression of the disease, we found moments of joy.

I remember taking Dad fishing with Cheryl. It was a bittersweet day — we were thrilled to be out on the water together, but Dad spent a lot of the time sleeping in the boat. It hurt to see the impact of his cancer on doing the thing he loved most.

There was another day on the Hawkesbury River when Cheryl, Kevin, Dad, and I went out fishing, and I somehow managed to fall out of the boat and capsize it completely.

We were all soaked, scrambling to rescue our gear, but even in the chaos, we laughed. That day reminded me that laughter and love are anchors, even in the middle of a storm.

The Hardest Prayer

In the final months, my emotions became conflicted.

I wanted as much time as possible with Dad, but watching him suffer was agonizing.

I started to pray for him to pass peacefully, even though it broke my heart to do so. It felt wrong to wish for the end, but at the same time, it was the kindest wish I could make for him.

Waiting for the inevitable was excruciating. There's something uniquely painful about knowing you're losing someone but having no control over when or how.

What I Learned from My Dad

Dad passed away on January 1, 2002. His death changed me in ways I never expected.

I learned that no one is promised tomorrow. The only time we truly have is the day we are living right now. That lesson gave me the strength and courage to pursue my dreams and start my own business a few years later.

And through it all, Dad's words continue to guide me:

"It's all good!"

He said it all the time. No matter what was happening, he would find the silver lining. During a cyclone, he'd celebrate the calm of the eye. When things went wrong, he'd encourage us to look for what we could learn.

I carry that with me to this day. "It's all good" and hence the title of my book.

Shaping My Approach to Life and Challenges

Dad's cancer taught me to remove emotions from events.

The meaning I assign to an event is entirely up to me. The event itself holds no power—I decide what it means. This perspective allows me to step off the emotional roller coaster, avoiding the sharp drops and dizzying highs. I still feel joy, pain, fear, and happiness, but now it's more like riding the kiddies' roller coaster—gentler, steadier—rather than the wild, heart-pounding rides of my youth.

I also learned that other people's behavior is on them, not me.

There were people who clung so rigidly to their rules during Dad's illness that they lost sight of compassion. When Dad asked for anointing from his long-term church, he was denied—because he ate clean meat. Eating clean meat was within the church's teachings, but the elders at the time decided that this choice made him "not right with God." And if he was right with God, they reasoned, he would be cancer free.

When Dad returned to Sydney, the church ministers there welcomed him with open arms and anointed him without hesitation. But I don't think he ever fully recovered from the wound of rejection by his home church.

For a long time, I carried deep bitterness over their actions. But eventually, I realized that holding on to resentment only hurt me.

Now, I choose to move on. I choose love and grace over bitterness.

Making Peace with God

I was raised in a religious family and had a wonderful childhood. We were taught to pray, to ask for God's blessings, and to trust in His plan. But when Dad got sick, I found myself wrestling with what that truly meant.

To me, praying for healing meant that Dad would be the <1% who survived. That was the blessing I wanted. But what I came to understand was that God's definition of blessings and mine were not the same. Healing did come for Dad—just not in the way I had hoped. His earthly journey ended here, but that didn't mean my prayers weren't heard or that God had abandoned us.

I've come to believe that God walks with us for however long our journey lasts. His love doesn't falter, even when life doesn't go the way we desperately want it to. Faith, I learned, isn't about getting the answer you ask for—it's about knowing you are not alone, no matter what that answer turns out to be.

And if your diagnosis is terminal, do not let anyone tell you that means you are not right with God. That belief is ignorance, not faith, and it has no place in your journey. Shame on those who seek to shame you. God loves you. Believe in that!

Finding Strength in Myself

In the years after Dad's passing, I committed to personal development and building a strong foundation of self-belief and ethics.

I've learned to face challenges head-on, to remove fear from my decision-making, and to live by the principle of:

"What meaning am I choosing to give this?"

I still miss Dad every day, and the hole in my heart is healing. His wisdom and love are still with me — in the way I approach life, in the way I treat others, and in the way I lead my business.

And through it all, his voice echoes in my mind:

"It's all good!"

REFLECTIONS FOR YOU

If you're navigating a challenging time, here are some insights from my journey that may help you:

1. Life is lived one day at a time.

You're not promised tomorrow. Focus on today and make it count.

2. You choose the meaning you give events.

An event holds no meaning until you assign one to it. Choose a meaning that serves you, not one that weighs you down.

3. It's okay to feel conflicted emotions.

You can want more time with someone and still wish for their peace. Both feelings are valid.

PROJECT LOVING LUMPY — REFRAMING CANCER WITH HUMOR AND LOVE

$\mathcal{M}$y Original Post

HI FRIENDS.

I was expecting the words, "It's cancer," but it was still a shock. I'm pretty good at reading people, and there was a subtle shift in the various doctors and technicians involved in my scans and biopsy that clued me in that I may soon be checking the box next to "cancer" on my medical forms.

And sure enough, a day after the news, I was having a CT scan of my head and neck and putting a check against that box!

But let me step back and give you some backstory about how I came to join the cancer group.

I found a small but growing lump on my upper right jaw in October 2022. It was not painful, and initially, I thought it was a cyst. I was busy seeing a raft of specialists and technicians for my upcoming total knee replacement surgery and didn't see my GP about the lump until early December 2022. I cannot pinpoint any one thing that urged me to go to the doctor; it was just a feeling that the lump was "something."

(Side note: Always listen to your still, small voice inside. It knows things!)

An ultrasound followed, showing "suspicious characteristics," and then there was a five-week wait over Christmas for an ultrasound-guided biopsy, which resulted in a malignant tumor diagnosis. For those who like details, I have parotid squamous cell carcinoma — a malignant tumor in my salivary gland.

I've never had a cancer diagnosis before, and as confronting as it is, I'm taking each day as it comes and focusing on my life as a whole. I will say, though, that I've been remarkably calm during the last nine weeks, and that surprised me. I always figured I'd be the one to fall apart, but it's like I have this center of calm that knows I'll be okay no matter what happens.

My approach is not to "battle" or "fight" cancer; instead, I'm just Loving Lumpy (yes, I named my lump). There's so much expectation put on "fighting the good fight" or "being cured." I say, let's skip expectations and the "shoulds"! It's fair to say that this "should" not be happening — but it is, and I'm going to love Lumpy and stay in the day I'm in.

So far, I've had two malignant diagnoses for this tumor, so I was surprised when Dr. ENT said the pathology might be wrong and suggested a third test diagnosis (PET scan). Obviously, anything is possible, and things can change on the turn of a coin — hence why living in the day I'm in is so important.

The PET scan showed that Lumpy is a primary cancer (not secondary or metastatic — yay!), contained with no fingerlings branching out, and not in my lymph nodes.

I've made this group because I want to share my journey with my FB friends, but my wall doesn't feel like the right place to do that. I'm happy for others to join the group or be recommended by you. I welcome, with open arms and heart, all the love, prayers, faith, positive thoughts, wisdom, and sharing you can offer! Some of you may have had similar experiences and can share your unique perspectives with me.

I also know that broader conversations will help center me, too, so don't feel this group needs to be just about me and Loving Lumpy. Lumpy doesn't need that much attention, lol. Feel free to ask me what I'm celebrating today or about my trip to Katmai National Park to see the bears and salmon migration in August 2024. Or my return visit to beautiful Banff in Alberta, Canada.

Heads up: There may be times when I'm quiet or when I ignore you if you ask how I'm doing. It really isn't you; it's me. We all have those days when we need time out, so please don't worry if I take a little time to respond.

My plan is to continue working — because I've got a big hairy audacious goal in my sights! — but also to keep myself centered and grounded.

Thank you for your friendship, love, support, and sharing.

Please join me in Loving Lumpy. 🤍

REFLECTIONS

Looking back, that first message marked a pivotal moment for me. It wasn't just about telling people I had cancer; it was about setting the tone for how I wanted to navigate this experience.

I've always believed that language matters. The words we choose shape our thoughts and emotions. By choosing to frame my journey as "Loving Lumpy" instead of "fighting cancer," I took control of the narrative. I wasn't a victim; I was an active participant in my healing process.

And that simple decision made all the difference.

2ND NOTE ABOUT DIAGNOSIS

For those who love details, here's a bit more about the type of cancer I have: parotid squamous cell carcinoma.

The parotid is your salivary gland, running down each side of your face. All your facial nerves pass through it, from your ear to your eyebrows, nose, cheeks, mouth, etc.

I've had two ultrasounds and a fine needle biopsy, which confirmed the type of cancer.

Parotid cancer is uncommon — making up about 5% of all head and neck cancers.

Malignant primary parotid cancers are even more uncommon, with only 20% being malignant. Usually, parotid lumps are benign.

And then there's my type of cancer: squamous cell carcinoma, typically a type of skin cancer. It's rare to find it in the parotid as a primary cancer. Usually, it's secondary, with the primary tumor located somewhere on the head, neck, or brain.

A CT scan of my neck, head, and brain showed no other cancers. Yay me!

Still, my ENT doctor wasn't convinced about the pathology, so he ordered a PET scan, which is a deep, whole-body scan to check for anything lurking elsewhere.

The PET scan confirmed that the cancer is primary and contained, with no other abnormalities or issues in my body. Double yay me!

Next, I'll meet with my multidisciplinary health team and then my surgeon for a one-on-one consult.

REFLECTIONS

I learned early on that knowledge is power, and that has been a recurring theme in my approach to life challenges. By understanding my diagnosis thoroughly, I took some of the mystery — and fear — out of it.

This also allowed me to make decisions based on facts, not emotions. The more I understood the medical details, the calmer I became.

This mindset can be helpful for anyone facing a health scare: Ask questions. Stay informed. Don't be afraid to seek a second (or third) opinion.

REFLECTIONS: REFRAMING THE NARRATIVE

When I was first diagnosed with parotid cancer, I knew I'd be facing one of the biggest challenges of my life. But I also knew one thing: I didn't want to hide from it or give it power over me.

So, I named my tumor Loving Lumpy.

Let me be clear — I'm terrible at naming things. I'm literal by nature, and since it was a lump, Lumpy seemed as good a name as any.

I did throw around a few more creative names with friends, but nothing really grabbed me. So, Lumpy it was.

But the name became so much more than a joke. It became a mindset. It set the tone for how I wanted to approach my cancer — with honesty, lightness, and above all, love.

Shedding Light on Fear

I've always believed that when you shine a light on something difficult — something you fear or hate — you take away its power.

Naming my tumor Lumpy was a way of shining that light. It turned something scary and unknown into something manageable, something I could talk about without flinching.

I didn't want to shy away from the fact that I had cancer, but I also didn't want to walk around saying "my parotid cancer" all the time. That just felt a bit too clinical and impersonal.

Naming the tumor made it less scary. It helped me accept it, and it made it easier for others to talk about, too.

Friends would ask, "How's Loving Lumpy doing?"

That's a much softer, more approachable question than, "How's your parotid cancer?" The name opened the door for connection and conversation.

Love Over Fear

One of the most surprising things about naming my tumor Loving Lumpy was how it set the tone for the entire cancer journey.

It wasn't intentional, but the name itself infused love into the process.

Love over fear. Love over anger. Love over despair.

Cancer is often framed as a battle or a fight, but I didn't want to approach it that way. It felt exhausting to imagine myself in constant combat mode against my own body.

Instead, I chose to accept it. Not to give up, but to welcome it as part of my experience. And when you name something, it's hard to fight it.

Sharing the Journey

Cheryl encouraged me to document my journey through a private Facebook group.

At first, I wasn't sure I wanted to do it. Sharing something so personal and vulnerable with others wasn't something I was naturally inclined to do. Plus, who would be interested? Lots of people have cancer.

But once I started sharing, I realized it was a way to process my experience and connect with others.

The name Loving Lumpy set the tone from the start. It made the updates less formal, less clinical, and more approachable.

People were able to ask questions and offer support without feeling awkward or unsure of what to say. The love and humor in the name created a space where we could talk about something scary in a way that felt human.

What Naming Lumpy Taught Me

Looking back, I realize that naming the tumor taught me some important lessons about acceptance, mindset, and communication.

1. Acceptance doesn't mean giving up.

Naming Lumpy wasn't about resigning myself to cancer. It was about acknowledging reality and choosing to approach it with love rather than fear.

2. Reframing changes the emotional weight.

By reframing cancer as Lumpy, I shifted it from something terrifying to something I could talk about more easily. That reframe changed how I experienced it — and how others around me did, too.

3. Connection is healing.

Naming the tumor made it easier for friends and family to connect with me. They weren't sure how to ask about parotid cancer, but they could ask about Loving Lumpy. And that connection was part of my healing.

KEY TAKEAWAYS FOR YOU

Here's what my experience taught me — and what I'd love for you to take with you:

1. You get to choose how you frame your challenges.

Life will throw unexpected things at you. You can't always control what happens, but you can control how you interpret it. Reframing your narrative can make all the difference.

2. Find your calm center.

For me, it's about staying present and taking each day as it comes. Instead of worrying about "what ifs," I focus on what's in front of me right now.

3. Lean on your community.

I created a Facebook group to share my journey with friends, and the love and support I received made a huge difference. You don't have to go through challenges alone.

A PRACTICAL TAKEAWAY FOR YOU

If you're facing something scary, overwhelming, or unknown, here's a simple exercise to help you reframe it and take away some of its power:

1. Name it.

Whether it's an illness, a fear, or a challenge, give it a name that feels less intimidating. It doesn't have to be clever — just something that makes it feel more manageable.

2. Acknowledge it.

By naming it, you're shining a light on it. You're saying, "I see you. I acknowledge you."

3. Choose how you want to engage with it.

Do you want to fight it? Accept it? Find humor in it? Love it? Whatever you choose, know that you get to decide the emotional tone of your experience.

4. Share your story.

If it feels right, share your journey with others. You never know who might be waiting to hear your story — and who might find comfort in your approach.

Love Is Always the Answer

In the end, Loving Lumpy wasn't just a name.

It was a philosophy. A way of saying that even in the hardest moments, love matters.

Love for yourself. Love for the people around you. Love for life — no matter how unpredictable or challenging it might be.

Because at the end of the day, it's all good.

Even when it doesn't feel that way, there's always love to be found.

FACTS ABOUT PAROTID — FACING THE UNKNOWN

❧

*M*y Original Post

•*5% of cancers are parotid.*

•*Five-year survival averages about 90%.*

[Source: https://pubmed.ncbi.nlm.nih.gov/30855924/]

•*In Australia, where the incidence of skin cancer is very high, metastasis (secondary spread) from facial skin cancer — especially squamous cell carcinoma, melanoma, and Merkel cell carcinoma — to lymph nodes around/within the parotid gland is common.*

[Source: http://www.drsydneychng.com.au/services/head-neck-surgery/parotid-tumors/]

A Personal Take on These Stats

When I first encountered these numbers, my immediate thought was, "I am rare! Ok, Loving Lumpy is rare!"

It felt strange to take comfort in the fact that my cancer was unusual. But I've learned that sometimes you have to find joy wherever you can — even in the oddest of places. And, well, being rare made me feel unique in a way that lightened the load.

The statistics painted a picture of both hope and reality.

- *5% of head and neck cancers are parotid cancers.*
- *Of that 5%, only 20% are malignant.*
- *Of that 20%, between 0.3% and 9.8% are squamous cell carcinoma.*

The math was clear: I was a statistical outlier. But to me, that was a reminder that no matter what odds you face in life, you can still find ways to reframe the narrative and take control of how you respond.

A Word of Warning: Know When to Stop

While understanding your diagnosis is empowering, there's a fine line between being informed and overwhelming yourself.

I've seen how easy it is to fall down a rabbit hole of endless research — and it can be detrimental to your mental health. The internet is awash with facts, real and imagined, and it's often hard to separate the two.

For me, I found comfort in sticking to trusted sources. My go-to was the Mayo Clinic, which provided accurate, up-to-date information that I could rely on.

But more than that, I made a conscious choice to avoid immersing myself too deeply in the details. I didn't need to read every forum or every article on parotid cancer. That wasn't going to change my outcome — it would only add to my anxiety.

So, my advice to anyone on a similar journey is this: be mindful of how much information you consume. Stay curious but grounded. And when you find yourself spiraling, step away from the research and refocus on living in the present.

REFLECTIONS

When I first felt the lump on the side of my face, I assumed it was a cyst.

It was hard, mobile, and felt like a pea. There was no pore opening, and I didn't feel unwell, so I thought it might be nothing serious.

But something about it made me pause.

Since I was a teenager, I've heard the message: "If you feel something like a pea, go to the doctor."

That advice was usually in reference to breast cancer checks, but this lump wasn't in my breast. It was on my face. Still, the texture and size triggered a gut feeling that this wasn't something to ignore.

Learning About the Parotid Gland

I wasn't even aware that there was such a thing as a parotid gland.

When I first noticed the lump, I did what many of us do these days: I Googled it. But I didn't want to go down the rabbit hole of random internet advice. I wanted trusted information.

So, I searched the Mayo Clinic website for "lump on the side of the face.

I wasn't expecting to see parotid cancer listed as one of the possibilities. There were also benign options — which I tried to focus on — but something about seeing "parotid cancer" stuck with me.

It was like a quiet whisper in my mind saying, "Prepare yourself."

The Scan and Diagnosis

When I saw my GP, he acted quickly. He's a great diagnostician and immediately sent me for a scan.

Within a day, I was in a clinic having my ultrasound.

I remember the Technician being kind and gentle, but I also remember seeing her body language change as she worked. When the results aren't good, there's always a shift — a little extra kindness, a softening of tone.

It's in those moments that you realize: "This might be serious."

Hearing the News

When my GP told me the results, he was blunt and to the point.

"It's cancer."

He was prepared with next steps — referrals and a treatment plan — and within minutes, I was out the door.

I sat in my car in the carpark, feeling a mix of laughter and tears. I think I laughed because it felt surreal, and I cried because the weight of the word "cancer" had finally landed.

But then, something inside me clicked.

I said out loud: "Okay, let's do this."

Telling My Family

The hardest part of that day was sharing the news with my family.

I called my sister and brother to give them a heads-up, and then I went home to tell Mum in person.

As I told her, I kept saying: "It's all good."

It was partly for her, but also for me. I was calm, I was present, and I knew that I had to set the tone for how we would approach this as a family.

Taking Action: A Way to Reclaim Control

One of the first things I realized after my diagnosis was that I needed to take action.

In Australia, we have socialized medicine, and I'd been referred to the public hospital system for follow-up. But it was December, and Christmas break was coming up. I knew that meant delays.

I didn't want to sit and wait with cancer inside me. I wanted it out.

So, I got a referral to a private doctor and paid to see him.

Taking action — even something as simple as booking an appointment — was incredibly helpful for my mental health. It felt like I was moving forward, rather than sitting in fear.

What I Learned About Facing a Diagnosis

Looking back, I've learned a few important lessons from that initial diagnosis:

1. Trust your gut.

If something doesn't feel right, get it checked out. Even if it's small or doesn't seem serious, pay attention to your body.

2. Find trusted sources of information.

Google wisely. Stick to reputable medical sites like the Mayo Clinic or Cancer Council and avoid forums or random blogs that can lead to unnecessary anxiety.

3. Take action to reclaim a sense of control.

Even small steps — like booking an appointment or asking for a second opinion — can make you feel more empowered in the face of something overwhelming.

4. Reframe the challenge.

Naming my tumor Lumpy helped me reframe the experience. It turned something frightening into something manageable.

A PRACTICAL TAKEAWAY FOR YOU

If you or someone you know is facing a serious diagnosis, here's a simple exercise to help you stay grounded and take back control:

1. Stick to trusted information.

Choose one or two reputable sources for medical information and ignore the rest.

2. Identify one action you can take.

Even a small action — like making an appointment or writing down questions — can help you feel more in control.

3. Name the challenge.

Give it a name that helps you feel less intimidated. Whether it's a health issue, a fear, or a life challenge, naming it can help you process and accept it.

MOVING FORWARD

In those early days, I didn't know what the future held. But I knew one thing:

It was all good.

Because no matter what came next, I was ready to face it with love, humor, and action.

FIRSTS

My Original Post

First Time:

•Crying in my business Mastermind and saying I didn't want to die (Thursday 15/12)

•Session with an Energy Practitioner (4/1)

•Ticking the box for cancer on a medical consent form (Friday 20/1)

•CT of head and neck checking for any cancer spread (Friday 20/1)

•Chatting with Susan about Lumpy, and we (make that, I) were normal (Saturday 21/1)

•Advance Health Directive filled out (Saturday 21/1)

•Clarity on my one thing I must do before I die (I will regret this if I don't do it): $1M biz

•Decided on Project Loving Lumpy and started sending love to my tumor

•Started my book — business, pragmatism, love & energy

•Felt certain for the first time that I am okay

•CT scan coming back clear (Monday 23/1)

•Face-to-face meeting with my team and sharing the news (Monday 23/1)

•Billing a client for a year-long 2023 project (Monday 23/1)

•Message from a Mastermind client who made me feel badass (Monday 23/1)

•Face-to-face meeting with a client's team and sharing the news (Tuesday 24/1)

•Meeting with an ENT Specialist (Tuesday 24/1)

•Meeting with the Townsville University Hospital's ENT Unit Registrar (Wednesday 1/2/23)

•PET scan (Friday 3/2/23)

•Private Specialist rang me at home to give PET results (Monday 6/2/23)

•Visit to Townsville University Hospital's Cancer Unit (Tuesday 7/2/23)

•Townsville University Hospital's Multidisciplinary Team meeting (Tuesday 7/2/23)

REFLECTIONS: CELEBRATING FIRSTS

We tend to focus on lasts — the last time we'll do something or see someone. But what I've learned is that firsts are just as important. They represent new beginnings, new ways of thinking, and new ways of showing up in the world. I remember sitting in the Hospital's coffee shop early on in 2023 as I waited for my next meeting. I had four that day with different specialities. I remember thinking that here's goes another first and that I should record all my firsts as something fun to do and as a way to reframe them into a fist pump moment.

It's easy to overlook small wins just in the everyday event of living, but when we're going through something tough, small wins can disappear into the ether. But I've found that celebrating each first — no matter how small — helps me stay grounded and keeps me moving forward.

KEY TAKEAWAYS FOR YOU

Here are a few things I've learned about firsts that might be helpful for you:

1. Firsts are new beginnings.

Every first, even the hard ones, represents a step forward. Embrace them for what they are — a sign of growth and progress.

2. Celebrate your wins.

Don't wait for the big milestones to celebrate. Every small win counts. Whether it's a good medical report or simply making it through a tough day, take a moment to acknowledge your progress.

3. Allow yourself to be human.

There's no right or wrong way to go through a challenging time. Give yourself grace and permission to feel all the emotions that come with those firsts.

A PRACTICAL TAKEAWAY FOR YOU

If you're navigating a difficult season in life, try this exercise to track and celebrate your firsts:

1. Start a "Firsts" journal.

Write down every new thing you experience during this time. It could be something big, like a major surgery, or something small, like the first time you laugh after a difficult day. I created mine in the Notes app on my phone, so it was easy to update.

2. Reflect on each first.

Ask yourself: What did this moment teach me? How did it make me feel? What did I learn about myself?

3. Celebrate your wins.

Take time to celebrate your progress. It doesn't have to be a big celebration — even a quiet acknowledgment can make a difference.

OPERATION DUMPING LUMPY - PREPARING FOR SURGERY WITH INTENTION AND RESILIENCE

$$\mathscr{CB}$$

$\mathcal{M}$y Original Post

TODAY'S THE DAY!!! *I am breaking up with Loving Lumpy!!!*

Thank you, Loving Lumpy, for the insights you brought, but ultimately, it's time for us to part. Bye bye, Lumpy!

Sitting in the Operating Theatre waiting room with my brother and sister, I am reminded that the body doesn't lie. I thought I was cool, calm, and collected, all ready for surgery. But after peeing for the sixth time in two hours, Kevin finally clued me in — all those visits to the restroom were my body's way of telling me I was nervous, and that I should listen to it!

There's nowhere to hide from yourself!

To my family, friends, clients, and team, thank you for your prayers, super dooper mojo, light, and love as I head into surgery (it will be 3-4 hours long) and afterward as I heal.

Here I go! 🤍

REFLECTIONS ON SURGERY DAY

Looking back on this day, what stands out most is how calm and confident I felt leading up to the surgery — or at least, that's what I thought.

In the days leading up to it, I realized there was still a knot of uncertainty sitting quietly in the back of my mind. I was nervous — not about the surgery itself, but about what they might find.

The doctors were taking a conservative approach. They would remove the tumor and a few nearby lymph nodes and then send the nodes to Pathology. If they found cancerous cells, I'd need a second surgery to remove more lymph nodes from my neck.

I was cranky about that.

Why not just take the lymph nodes out during the first surgery and get it over with?

But no — it didn't happen that way.

Setting Intentions for Surgery

I couldn't control how the doctors would approach my case, but I knew I could control my own mindset.

So, every morning and night in the weeks before my surgery, I practiced visualization.

I didn't waste time imagining that the cancer wasn't real or that it hadn't spread. That felt pointless to me as the cancer would be whatever and wherever it was. Instead, I focused on how I wanted to be.

I visualized:

• Waking up in Recovery feeling calm and safe.

• Interacting positively with the nurses and doctors caring for me.

• Healing quickly and getting out of the hospital as soon as possible.

My goal wasn't to change the external reality. It was to influence my internal state so that I could handle whatever came my way with grace and calm.

Breathing Through It

I've always found that deep breathing helps me stay calm, so I made it part of my preparation.

Every day, I practiced deep meditative breathing, knowing that once I was in the hospital, I'd use it to stay grounded and relaxed.

It became a natural tool for me — something I could reach for in moments of anxiety.

The Reality of Surgery Day

Despite all my preparation, the morning of my surgery was a bit of a reality check.

In reality, my body was screaming what my mind was trying to ignore: "You're scared."

It's funny how we can fool ourselves into thinking we're fine when our bodies know better. My repeated trips to the restroom were my body's way of processing the anxiety that my mind was trying to push away. I've learned that the body never lies. It knows what we're feeling, even if we're trying to convince ourselves otherwise.

Still, it wasn't panic or dread — just natural levels of worry. The kind of nervous energy anyone would feel before going under the knife.

Also, I was still feeling my way in what 'normal' concern felt like as opposed to unvoiced fear or dread. Once I recognised what was going on with all the visits to the restroom, I then had a gauge between healthy and unhealthy worry.

My Process for Handling Fear

In the week leading up to surgery, I did something that has always helped me: I mapped out my worst-case scenarios.

I wrote down every fear and what could go wrong, and then I drilled down into what the consequences might be.

It's a process that looks something like this:

1. What if they find cancer has spread to my lymph nodes?

•They'll remove those cancerous nodes surgically.

2. What if the cancer can't be fully removed?

•I'll need chemo and radiation.

3. What if chemo and radiation work?

•I'll lose my hair during treatment.

4. What if they still can't kill the cancer?

•Death.

5. Am I ready for that?

•Death would suck as there's so much I still want to see in the world, but I am as ready as I can be.

Finding Peace Through Acceptance

That exercise — mapping out my worst fears and asking myself if I could live with each outcome — helped me find peace.

I realized that the only thing I truly feared was the unknown.

Once I'd named my fears and walked through each scenario, I was able to let go of much of my anxiety.

I accepted that I couldn't control everything, but I could control how I responded.

The Core of It All: Choosing Life

At the core of all my preparation was one simple truth:

I wanted to live.

And not just survive — I wanted to live well.

I was willing to do whatever it took to make that happen. Surgery, recovery, breathing exercises, visualizations — all of it.

This wasn't just about dumping Lumpy. It was about embracing life with both hands and saying, "I'm here for it all."

Breaking Up with Lumpy

Saying goodbye to Lumpy wasn't just about the physical act of surgery. It was a symbolic moment — a decision to let go of what no longer served me.

For months, Loving Lumpy had been a part of me. I had embraced it with love and acceptance, but this moment marked a turning point. It was time to release that chapter and step into the next phase of my journey.

Breaking up with Lumpy wasn't a declaration of war. It was an act of peace and gratitude. Lumpy had taught me valuable lessons about resilience, mindset, and living in the present moment. But now it was time to part ways.

A Word on Gratitude

As I sat in the waiting room with my brother and sister, I was deeply aware of the power of community. The prayers, love, and light I received from friends, family, and clients were more than just well-wishes. They were a source of strength that I carried with me into that operating room.

There's something profound about knowing that you're not alone — that there are people holding you in their hearts, even when you're about to face something scary. It reminded me that community and connection are some of the greatest gifts we have.

REFLECTIONS: SAYING GOODBYE WITH LOVE

"Operation Dumping Lumpy" wasn't a battle cry. It wasn't about fighting cancer or going to war with my body. Instead, it was about releasing what no longer served me with love and gratitude.

Loving Lumpy had been part of me for months, and while I was ready to say goodbye, I did so with an open heart. I thanked Lumpy for the lessons it taught me and let it go without fear or anger.

It was also a reminder that we don't have to face challenges alone. The love and support I received from friends, family, and my medical team made all the difference that day. I felt held, seen, and cared for.

KEY TAKEAWAYS FOR YOU

Here are some lessons I've learned about preparing for big challenges — whether it's surgery, a difficult conversation, or any major life event:

1. Letting go can be an act of love.

There are times we hold on to things that no longer serve us. Letting go — whether it's a fear, a mindset, or a relationship — can be an act of love and self-care.

2. You don't have to do it alone.

Lean on the people around you, including people you may not have even thought of. Whether it's friends, family, or a community, accepting help and support is a sign of strength, not weakness.

3. You can't control everything, but you can control how you show up.

Setting intentions isn't about changing reality — it's about deciding how you want to respond to it.

4. Deep breathing is a powerful tool.

Practicing calm, controlled breathing before a challenge makes it easier to access when you need it most.

5. Map out your worst fears.

Write down your worst-case scenarios and ask yourself if you can live with each outcome. You'll often find that naming your fears takes away their power.

A PRACTICAL TAKEAWAY FOR YOU

Here's a simple exercise you can try when preparing for a big challenge or stressful event:

1. Set your intentions.

Ask yourself: How do I want to be during this experience?

Visualize yourself how you want to be. For me, it was calm, focused, and grounded.

2. Practice deep breathing.

Spend a few minutes each day practicing calm, meditative breathing so it becomes second nature.

3. List your worst-case scenarios.

Write down your biggest fears and what could go wrong.

Drill down into each consequence until you reach the worst possible outcome.

Ask yourself: Can I live with that? If you cannot, what do you need to do, be or have in order to accept the worst outcome. There is immense freedom once fear is removed. Nor does it mean that the worst possible outcome is your outcome. All it means is that you have gifted yourself with peace.

4. Accept what you can't control.

Focus on what you can influence — your attitude, your response, and your actions.

5. Write a letter of gratitude to what you're letting go.

It could be a fear, a limiting belief, or even a challenging experience. Thank it for what it taught you, and then give yourself permission to release it.

6. Create a support list.

Write down the names of people or resources you can lean on when things feel hard. Knowing who to reach out to can bring comfort and reduce feelings of isolation.

7. Celebrate your milestones.

In this, size does not count! No matter how small a milestone, take time to acknowledge your progress. Each step forward is worth celebrating.

I hope this helps you see that letting go doesn't have to be painful. It can be an act of peace and love.

MOVING FORWARD WITH STRENGTH

The day of my surgery, I walked into that hospital knowing I was as ready as I could be.

I wasn't fearless, but I was prepared.

Because at the core of it all, I knew:

I wanted to live.

And that intention shaped every choice I made from that moment on.

AND I'M BACK — MINUS LUMPY!

*M*y Original Post

It's the day after Dumping Lumpy, and the surgical team has visited and given me an update. What a positive group they were. You know how some teams look like they'd rather be anywhere else? Not this team. Engaged. Happy. And they laughed at my jokes. 5 ⭐ for that. 😊

My surgery went well. Lumpy was removed encapsulated (fully contained with a full border of good tissue around it and no bits left behind). Lumpy is now off to Pathology, and we await the results — 1 to 2 weeks. Because the pathology and some of the tumor's presentation have been contrary, this result will be considered final!

Once the pathology results are back, I'll know my next steps. I'm ready for whatever those are. 💪

Two small lymph nodes were removed from under my chin as a precaution since they were showing pre-cancer signs. They are off to Pathology too for a diagnosis.

My wound is pain-free, although the right jawline and tooth crown on that side are sore from where they had to tunnel along to reach the lymph nodes! I'm just on Panadol (Tylenol) and ibuprofen, and that's managing things well.

My wound is a thing of beauty, even in its newness. The ENT doc does fine work! (I asked, and he did the close.)

All my nerves, except my earlobe, have been preserved — they all work! Praise the Lord! Hallelujah! I can blink, smile, bite over my bottom lip, bite over my top lip, frown, scrunch up my face, wriggle my nose, puff my cheeks out, and talk. Yay me!!!

If I had one fear with this surgery, it was losing my ability to speak as I do now. I make my living speaking, so there's that. But more than anything, I think it reminded me of the despair I felt when my Dad lost the ability to speak due to his brain cancer.

However, Dad's story is not mine, and I'm happy to continue torturing everyone with my verbal views on everything.

And the wins keep coming...

My hair was not cut, so my hairdresser won't have to do a repair job. Woot woo!

Funny hair story: When Kevin (my brother) came to see me last night, he laughingly informed me I had "Something About Mary" hair because of all the surgery goop in my hair. Of course, it doesn't help that I can't wash my hair for a week! I'll just be styling the movie star look until then.

REFLECTIONS: CELEBRATING THE LITTLE THINGS

I've learned that gratitude doesn't have to be reserved for the big moments. It's just as important to celebrate the little things — like keeping your hair intact after surgery or being able to make people laugh.

It's easy to focus on what's going wrong, especially when you're dealing with a health challenge. But I've found that focusing on what's going right helps keep me grounded and hopeful.

Even something as simple as a numb ear became a source of laughter for me. I couldn't feel my earbud, which led to a funny moment of searching for it — only to realize it was already in my ear! 😊

These moments of humor and lightness have been essential to my healing journey. They remind me that life goes on, and joy is always available if you look for it.

KEY TAKEAWAYS FOR YOU

Here are a few lessons I've learned that I hope will be helpful for you:

1. Gratitude is powerful.

Don't wait for big milestones to feel grateful. Celebrate the small wins along the way — they're just as important.

2. Humor can lighten the heaviest loads.

Laughter has been a lifeline for me. It doesn't take away the hard stuff, but it makes it easier to carry.

3. Your story is still unfolding.

Surgery was a significant moment in my journey, but it wasn't the end of the story. Every day is a new chapter.

A PRACTICAL TAKEAWAY FOR YOU

If you're going through a challenging time, try this gratitude exercise to help shift your focus to what's going right:

1. Start a "Gratitude List" journal.

Each day, write down three things you're grateful for — no matter how small. It could be as simple as "I had a good cup of coffee" or "I laughed today."

2. Find humor in the hard stuff.

Look for moments of lightness in your day. Even in difficult times, there's usually something to smile about. Allow yourself to laugh — it's healing.

3. Celebrate your progress.

No matter where you are in your journey, take a moment to acknowledge how far you've come. Each step forward is worth celebrating.

That's my reflection on coming back minus Lumpy.

HOW LOVING LUMPY FLICKED THE SWITCH FOR ME — FINDING CLARITY AND TAKING CONTROL

◈

*M*y Original Post

JUST BEFORE OUR *December Leverage meeting, I received a parotid cancer diagnosis. That first week, I was in shock, as those in the Leverage meeting could see.*

My mind went to death, as often happens with a cancer diagnosis, and I asked myself: What one thing would I want to achieve if I had limited time? This question literally changed everything for me.

Answers I had heard from others were things like spending more time with family and friends or traveling. But those didn't feel right to me. I already have healthy and happy relationships, and that wasn't going to change. I've traveled extensively, and while I have more countries to visit, travel wasn't THE priority.

My one thing is to grow a million-dollar-plus business because I know the impact I would bring to fiction authors and their dreams of writing full-time. What a legacy to leave behind!

And with that realization, all my fears dropped away.

In what has been a tumultuous 12 weeks, I've been happy and at peace. The closest description is a lightness of being.

I stopped apologizing for wanting my goal. It's my goal, and that's all that matters. I started appreciating myself for my brilliance and experienced a 180-degree turnaround in strength of perspective and purpose.

My business fears disappeared because I realized I already know what I need to do. I just hadn't been doing it. I am now, so watch me grow!

I met with an Energy Practitioner to help me center myself. I took time out to look at my business from the perspective of a million-dollar business owner, instead of a fearful but hopeful six-figure business owner.

I reviewed the workload of each team member, and then we got together and threw out the busy work and replaced it with activities tied directly to income and customer service.

I realized I was the roadblock in my business and delegated 70% of my workload. Now, when we create processes, it's without me in them. My focus now is lead generation and coaching.

The team is over the moon with their new responsibilities and has blown me away with their passion, initiative, and sense of self.

I called my cancer Loving Lumpy because I loved the gift it brought me. I wasn't going to fight it or battle it. I threw out the expectations of "benign" or "malignant" and just focused on loving each day for the gift it is.

"Operation Dumping Lumpy" surgery was this week. Bye-bye, Lumpy, you're out of here! And it is!

I'm doing really well. The entire tumor was cleanly removed, and two lymph nodes were taken out without issues. I retained all but one of my facial nerves, and I can talk, smile, frown, wink, puff out my cheeks, and wiggle my nose. Sweet!

I've been laughing at myself as I get used to the fact that my right ear is now numb. It still hears (yay!), but there's no feeling in the external ear since that facial nerve was cut. I spent minutes today searching for my earbud, only to discover it was in my numb ear, and I couldn't feel it! Too funny! 😄

It took a cancer diagnosis for me to take fearless action. I pray it's a nudge for you and not a brick like it was for me, but no matter what your nudge is: TAKE FEARLESS ACTION.

REFLECTIONS: FINDING CLARITY AND PURPOSE

When I first discovered the lump on my face, I didn't immediately think, "This is cancer."

I thought it might be a cyst or something benign. But deep down, something about it niggled at me.

I knew it wasn't nothing.

What I didn't know, though, was that this lump would change everything — not just my health, but how I approached my entire life.

A Defining Question

At the time of my diagnosis, I was part of a business mastermind program, where we met on Zoom every quarter for a two-day live training session.

One of those sessions happened right after my diagnosis, and the facilitator asked a question of the group that hit me hard:

"What's the one thing you would want to achieve if you had limited time?"

That question — paired with the reality of my own mortality — created a gigantic mental shift for me. I remember literally taking a deep breath as though I had been hit in the chest!

I'd always thought of terminally ill people writing down things like:

•Spend more time with family.

•Go on one last trip.

So that's what I wrote down first.

But when I looked at those answers, they didn't feel right.

I love my family, and I love travel, but those weren't the things calling to me.

Instead, I realized what I really wanted:

I wanted to build a million-dollar business.

A Childhood Dream, Reframed

The idea of having a million-dollar business has been with me since childhood.

Back then, it was about what a million dollars could buy me — a house, a car, financial freedom.

But now, it's about what that million dollars represents.

I realized that if my business was generating a million dollars, it meant I was changing the lives of my clients all over the world. It meant that those changes were rippling out beyond my clients — to their families, their communities, and beyond.

The dream wasn't about money anymore. It was about impact.

Take Time to Sit With Your Decision

I had the hardest time sharing my goal with others as I felt I would be judged negatively. In fact, I rarely shared it outside of a select few for the first twelve months. Whatever your one thing is, it is yours. You do not need to validate it with others or gain their approval. You do not even need to share it with others. It is up to you whether you share it or not.

If your 'one big thing' makes you feel uncomfortable-like mine did for months- keep it to yourself (or share it with a select few) and just sit with it. Spend time each day teasing out your idea. Have fun with it. Play with it. Each time you do that, you embrace it more and bring it into yourself more until it is such a natural part of yourself, outside opinion can no longer touch it.

Control What You Can: Your Attitude

One thing I knew from watching my dad and sister go through cancer was that there would be times when I would feel completely out of control.

I couldn't control:

•The treatment.

•The side effects.

•What the scans would show.

But I could control one thing:

My attitude.

So, I set clear expectations — for myself, my family, and my friends — about how I was going to handle this.

I wasn't going to "fight" cancer or "battle" it.

I wasn't going to frame it as an ordeal or horrific experience.

Instead, I decided to live each day as it came and do everything in my power to live well for as long as possible.

Setting My Terms

Just like my dad set expectations as kids when we went fishing, I set my own terms for how I wanted to approach cancer and its treatment.

And I let people know:

•Be positive.

•Live in the present.

•Be grateful.

•Laugh often.

That's how I wanted to live through this experience.

Not Everyone Got It

The first thing I noticed after setting these expectations was that not everyone could honor them.

Some struggled with my humor and asked if I realized how serious things were.

People still used words like "battle" and "fight."

They called me "brave" and said I was going through a "horrific ordeal."

Those words felt wrong to me.

I didn't see it as a battle. I wasn't fighting. I wasn't going through something horrific.

It made me stop and think:

Where in my own life was I failing to honor other people's expectations?

That realization led to another shift:

I realized that everyone comes to difficult situations with their own mindset and language. Some people frame things as fights or battles because that's how they process them. And that is typically the language used around cancer.

It taught me to be more mindful of other people's language and expectations, while still holding firm boundaries around my own experience.

The Power of a Mindset Shift

Naming my tumor Lumpy wasn't just about making it less scary.

It was about taking control of the narrative.

When I chose how to think about my diagnosis, I was choosing how to live through it.

REFLECTIONS FOR YOU

Here are some questions I encourage you to reflect on if you're facing a difficult situation or feeling stuck in life:

1. What's one thing you'd want to achieve if you had limited time?

•Be honest with yourself. What truly matters to you?

2. What can you control in this situation?

•You may not be able to control what happens, but you can control how you respond.

3. What terms or expectations can you set for yourself and others?

•How do you want to show up in this experience?

•How do you want others to engage with you?

KEY TAKEAWAYS FOR YOU

Here's what I've learned from this experience that I hope can help you:

1. Clarity creates momentum.

When you get clear on what truly matters to you, everything else falls into place. Your actions become aligned with your purpose.

2. Fearless action is the key to growth.

There will always be an element of fear, but it doesn't have to define your actions or control you. Take action anyway. It's in the doing that you'll find confidence and peace.

3. Your mindset shapes your reality.

How you think about yourself and your goals matters. When I started seeing myself as a million-dollar business owner, my decisions and actions changed.

A PRACTICAL TAKEAWAY FOR YOU

If you're feeling stuck or unsure about your next steps, try this exercise to gain clarity and take fearless action:

1. Ask yourself: What's the one thing I want to achieve?

Be honest. What's the one thing that, if left undone, you would regret the most?

2. Identify what's holding you back.

Is it fears. Self-doubt? Other people's expectations? Get them out of your head and write them down onto paper. Once you see them written down, you'll realize that many of them are less scary than they seem.

3. Find solutions for your core fear.

What's the worst that could happen? And if it did happen, what options would you have? When you have options, you have peace.

4. Take one small step today.

Don't wait for the perfect time. Take a small, fearless action today that moves you closer to your goal.

5. Set your terms.

Write down how you want to approach this goal.

Decide what language you'll use to frame your experience.

6. Communicate your expectations.

Let others know how to support you in this journey.

MOVING FORWARD WITH CLARITY

For me, cancer flicked a switch. I hope this book inspires you to flick your own switch and step into fearless action.

It made me realize that I didn't have time to play at my goals or get stuck in fear.

I had to shed the expectations of others and focus on what truly mattered to me.

Because at the end of the day, I knew:

It's all good.

And I was going to make it even better.

STORYTELLING — HOW SHARING MY JOURNEY CHANGED EVERYTHING

My Original Post

MY RECOVERY CONTINUES to go well. Sleeping through the night is still my biggest challenge, as I inevitably roll over onto my right side and, ouch!

I'm listening to my nursing team and taking the time to rest and recover. While I look and feel fine, it's important to remember that I've just had a four-hour surgery.

I've had a few questions about how I discovered Loving Lumpy, and in my favor, I caught it early.

Sharing our stories is so important. I saw this with my sister Cheryl and her Keep Smiling group when she was diagnosed with breast cancer in 2018. So, I thought I'd share my Loving Lumpy discovery story in case it inspires you to get something checked.

Loving Lumpy showed up one day, and initially, I thought it was a cyst. So, I put it out of my mind and focused on all the things around my upcoming knee replacement surgery.

Then in November, I read an update about John Farnham's cancer battle. John Farnham is Australia's best singer. I have been a fan since forever and loved going to his concerts. Like so many in Australia, I was deeply saddened when John was diagnosed with oral cancer in August 2022.

The reminder of his story of finding a small lump on his face was the impetus for me to go to my doctor. John was resistant at first, thinking it was nothing, but fortunately, his wife encouraged him to see someone. It turns out his lump was oral cancer and he underwent surgery to remove the tumour and part of his jaw, followed by radiation and reconstructive surgery.

Loving Lumpy was just a small lump. It didn't hurt. It didn't cause me any distress. It didn't bother me. But, what it was, was unusual.

I don't share nearly enough, but I'm changing that this year because I've seen the power of storytelling. Just this week, I was moved to discover two of my clients were motivated to go to their doctors because of my experience with Loving Lumpy.

My suggestion?

See your doctor when you feel off and notice something unusual.

•Do your annual breast mammogram.

•Do your bi-annual bowel cancer screening.

•Get your bits tested.

Just get checked.

NOTE: For my non-Aussie friends, John Farnham is one of the best singers in the world! I'm biased, but wrap your listening ears around these:

•The Voice (his signature song): https://youtu.be/tbkOZTSvrHs

•Collection of his first hits: https://youtube.com/playlist?list=PLtki-dVaa JTXYPfPSZChgL6bTReWXaBtb

REFLECTIONS: WHY STORYTELLING MATTERS

When I was diagnosed with parotid cancer, the last thing on my mind was sharing my story.

Cancer isn't uncommon, and I didn't feel like I had anything unique to say.

There are bazillions of people out there going through similar experiences, and I wasn't convinced that anything I said would be new or interesting.

But my sister, Cheryl, thought differently.

She had gone through her own cancer journey and had created a Facebook group to share her updates.

She convinced me that it would be good for me — and others — to do the same.

Plus, it was John Farnham's story about finding his mouth cancer diagnosis that was the push I needed to see my doctor about the lump on my face. John's story made a difference in my life — and now I've seen how my story has made a difference in the lives of others.

Why I Started Sharing My Story

At first, I agreed for purely practical reasons.

I remembered how draining it was to call, message, or email updates to individual people during my dad's cancer journey.

There's only so many times you can repeat the same news, and it becomes emotionally exhausting.

I thought, Why not put all the updates in one place?

It made sense to start a group where people could get the latest information, instead of me having to repeat myself over and over.

I didn't start it right away, though.

I waited until I had all the facts.

So, I created a private Facebook group on February 9th, after I had confirmation of my diagnosis.

I've always preferred to process information first, and then share once I have clarity.

Surprised by the Response

At first, I worried that no one would join.

It felt a bit like throwing a party and wondering if anyone would turn up.

But thankfully, family, friends, and colleagues were interested and engaged.

What surprised me most, though, was the depth of the interactions.

I've always been a writer, and I'm not afraid to share deeply personal thoughts and emotions.

But what I thought was just me sharing my feelings turned out to be something more.

People started commenting on my ability to articulate what I was feeling.

I wasn't expecting that.

I was just being me.

The Power of Vulnerability

Here's a comment that really stuck with me:

"God, your ability to articulate the minutiae of the thought processes and the immense tumultuous range of emotion experienced is just beyond the pale: you have a whole book here. Just really sorry you are the person having to do the 'experiencing' but adore your ability to convey in everyday language the immensity of the feelings. Sending much love 🤍*"*

Reading that comment, something clicked for me.

I realized that telling my story wasn't just helping me — it was helping others too.

Another comment that warmed my heart was this:

"I'm grateful for your ability to articulate your trajectory so vividly and for the reminder to get back into a daily routine of 'mindset work.' Thank you, my friend."

Why Storytelling Matters

Before I started sharing my journey, I hadn't really considered the impact of storytelling as it related to me.

But now I see that sharing our stories is how we connect as humans.

It's how we make sense of our experiences, process our emotions, and find meaning in difficult times.

When we share openly and honestly, we create space for others to do the same.

And when we name our fears and emotions, we take away some of their power.

KEY TAKEAWAYS FOR YOU

If you're going through a challenging time, I encourage you to consider sharing your story — even if it's just with a small group of trusted friends or family.

Here's what I've learned about storytelling:

1. You don't have to be an expert.

• You don't need to have all the answers or say something new.

• Your experience matters simply because it's yours. And never let anyone tell you your experience is right or wrong - it's YOUR experience.

2. Vulnerability creates connection.

•When you open up and share your true feelings, you give others permission to do the same.

3. You never know who needs to hear your story.

•Your words might inspire, comfort, or motivate someone in ways you never expected.

A PRACTICAL TAKEAWAY FOR YOU

If you're ready to share your story, here's a simple way to get started:

1. Choose your medium.

•It could be a private Facebook group, a blog, a YouTube channel, a journal, or even just talking with a friend.

2. Start with what you know.

•You don't need to tell the whole story at once.

•Start with what's happening right now and let the rest unfold naturally.

3. Focus on connection, not perfection.

•Your story doesn't need to be perfect.

•What matters most is being real and authentic.

MOVING FORWARD WITH PURPOSE

Starting my Facebook group wasn't about seeking attention or trying to be inspirational.

It was about finding a practical way to keep people informed.

But it turned into something much bigger.

It became a place of connection, vulnerability, and mutual support.

It reminded me that our stories matter — not just to us, but to the people we share them with.

And if there's one thing I've learned, it's this:

You never know who needs to hear your story.

UPDATE MARCH 15TH – 1ST VISIT SINCE SURGERY

My Original Post

TODAY WAS my first visit to my Specialist since my surgery. The two weeks since surgery have sped by!

Everything is healing nicely, and my scar continues to make an embroiderer proud! It's a thing of beauty! Looks like my career change to Pirate is off the cards!

They only had a partial pathology, which confirmed the squamous cell carcinoma finding from the biopsy. Possibly another week for the full pathology to be available.

The docs remain perplexed by the finding, but it looks like Loving Lumpy really is that super rare parotid cancer type. On this occasion, I would have been okay with being ordinary — lol!

A neck dissection surgery is in my immediate future, and three lymph nodes will be removed from under my neck. This is in addition to the two lymph nodes removed from under my chin during the tumor surgery.

Four weeks of radiation will follow after I've healed from that surgery.

So, I have the next steps in this little jaunt with Loving Lumpy, and it's comforting to have a plan.

How I'm Doing Mentally

Honestly? I'm doing great!

I did go into about 30 minutes of shock when the doc said a neck dissection was needed. I mean, I knew going into today's meeting that it was an option, but I was going to be the exception to the rule, right?! Ha!

I ride the same rollercoaster as others with similar health news, but my experience is more the kiddies' version rather than Six Flags.

I continue to focus on the day I'm in, and that makes a world of difference with my mindset.

I'm in good hands It's all good!

PS: It's no surprise to me that Ted Lasso returned to our screens today with season 3. Ted Lasso is the perfect mindset top-up for me! "Believe"

REFLECTIONS: THE POWER OF A PLAN

The two weeks after surgery went by in a bit of a blur.

Physically, I was recovering well. Emotionally, I felt calm and steady.

But I was keenly aware that my next doctor's visit would bring important answers.

I needed to know:

•What did the pathology results show?

•Was the tumor malignant?

•Had it spread to my lymph nodes?

•Would I need a second surgery?

I was ready for answers.

Seeking Clarity

Before my first surgery, the doctors had explained that a second surgery might be necessary to remove lymph nodes in my neck.

I remember feeling cranky about that.

Why not just take them all out in the first surgery?

I wasn't going to miss a few lymph nodes.

But as I thought about it more, I realized that doctors don't like to remove things unnecessarily. They know more about how the body works than I do, and there's no sense in removing healthy tissue if there's no clear need.

Still, I was eager to know:

- What exactly was Lumpy?
- Had it spread?
- And what was next?

Walking In with Intention

When the day of my first follow-up appointment arrived, I walked in feeling calm but curious.

I was reassured to see familiar faces among the medical team.

To prepare for this visit, I had gone through my notes from surgery and made a point to memorize the names of as many doctors and staff members as I could.

In the healthcare system, it's easy to feel like a number.

I knew from experience that being called by name matters.

So, I made sure to call them by their names.

I don't know if it made any difference to them, but it made a big difference to me.

It helped me feel seen — as a person, not just a patient.

Waiting for the Results

As I sat in the consultation room, I found myself hoping that the pathology results would confirm what the doctors had told me after surgery:

That the tumor had been removed encapsulated and that it hadn't spread.

But I also knew that hope wasn't a strategy.

I was prepared for whatever news came.

What mattered most to me was clarity — knowing exactly what I was dealing with and what the next steps would be.

The Importance of Feeling Seen

One thing I've learned through this journey is that the healthcare system can feel depersonalized.

It's not intentional, but when you're in a system that sees thousands of patients, it's easy to feel like just another file.

But we're not just files. We're people, with names, stories, and feelings.

So, I made a deliberate effort to connect with my healthcare team in a human way.

I don't know if calling them by name made a difference to how they treated me, but it helped me feel more grounded and seen.

A Little Help from Ted Lasso

I couldn't end this chapter without mentioning a perfect little coincidence that brought me a much-needed mindset top-up on the day of my hospital visit.

The new season of Ted Lasso was released that day.

If you haven't seen it, Ted Lasso is so much more than a tv show about football. It's about hope, kindness, forgiveness, and, above all, believing in yourself and others.

The values that run through Ted Lasso are cornerstones of my life too. The show's theme of "Believe" aligns beautifully with my journey.

Believing in:

•Myself.

•My care team.

•My ability to handle whatever comes next.

It was exactly the reminder I needed.

Because here's the thing about mindset work — it's not something you do once and then tick off the list.

We all need regular mindset top-ups to stay strong mentally.

For me, Ted Lasso has become one of those top-ups. It's a gentle nudge to keep believing in the good — even in difficult times.

And honestly? There's no better message to carry with you into a hospital visit than:

"Believe."

REFLECTIONS FOR YOU

If you're navigating a medical journey, here are some reflections to consider:

1. Clarity is powerful.

•When facing uncertainty, focus on getting clear answers.

•You can't control everything, but you can control how you prepare and respond.

2. Human connection matters.

•Even in large healthcare systems, small acts of human connection can make a difference.

•Learn the names of your doctors and nurses.

•Treat them as people, and you'll feel more like a person too.

3. Hope is important, but so is preparation.

•It's natural to hope for good news, but it's also important to prepare for all possibilities.

•Ground yourself in the present moment, and trust that you'll handle whatever comes next.

KEY TAKEAWAYS FOR YOU

Here are a few things I've learned from this experience that I hope will help you:

1. Plans bring peace.

Even when things don't go as expected, having a plan can provide a sense of control and calm.

2. Give yourself time to process.

It's okay to feel shocked or overwhelmed by unexpected news. Give yourself time to process your emotions before jumping into action.

3. Trust that you'll figure it out.

You don't need to know all the answers right away. Trust that you'll figure things out as you go — and lean on your support network when needed.

A PRACTICAL TAKEAWAY FOR YOU

If you're facing uncertainty or a big challenge, try this exercise to create a plan that brings peace:

1. Write down the steps you know you need to take.

Start with what you know for sure. Even a simple to-do list can bring clarity.

2. Identify the unknowns.

Acknowledge what you don't know yet. It's okay to have question marks.

3. Reach out for support.

Whether it's a friend, family member, or professional, don't be afraid to ask for help in making your plan.

4. Make a list of questions.

•What do you need clarity on?

•What answers are you hoping to receive?

5. Learn the names of the people you'll meet.

•Calling someone by name helps create connection and build trust.

6. Set your intention.

•Decide how you want to show up for this appointment.

•Do you want to be calm? Curious? Open to possibilities?

7. Practice grounding techniques.

•Use deep breathing or visualization to keep yourself present and centered.

MOVING FORWARD WITH CONFIDENCE

Walking into that first follow-up appointment, I realized that cancer hadn't taken away my control.

I could still control:

- How I prepared.
- How I interacted with others.
- How I responded to the news.

And I could control my attitude — choosing to see the human side of my medical journey and remain hopeful, even in uncertainty.

Because in the end, I knew:

It's all good.

HOW DID I GET TO BE SO CALM?
— FINDING BALANCE IN THE
CHAOS

❧

*M*y Original Post

I'VE HAD *a request from a couple of you asking, "How can you be so calm given everything going on?"*

I thought I would share my process with you in the hopes it may inspire you to adapt or use parts of it in your life. I use this in life and business, and it works for me and my personality.

Firstly, I believe that good and bad things happen to both good and bad people. So, something bad happening to me does not change my perspective of myself. I'm still a good person. 😇

Whenever I start a new work project or get major personal news like a cancer diagnosis, I do my "plan for the worst and expect the best" process to center myself and remove my fears.

Here's how it works:

1.Write Down Your Fears

I write down all the things I'm worried about. Seeing my fears on paper is cathartic. Some fears look silly once written down, while others are biggies that deserve more attention.

2.Identify Your Core Fear

I then figure out what my biggest fear is — the one that seems to have the most hold on me.

3.Search for Solutions

I set a timer and search for options or solutions in case things go pear-shaped. For health issues, I stick to trusted sources like the Mayo Clinic and Johns Hopkins to avoid medical rabbit holes. The timer keeps me focused on finding options rather than spiraling into doom and gloom.

Now, if the worst-case scenario plays out, I have options — and options equal peace.

Facing My Fears: Neck Dissection Example

When I learned I needed a neck dissection, I went through this process.

The doctor explained five possible side effects, including:

•Down-turned mouth

•Inability to shrug my right shoulder

•Diaphragm weakness

•Numb tongue

•Voice change

Of those, a droopy or down-turned mouth was my biggest fear. I wrote down all the bad things about it and realized that most were vanity issues.

For example:

•People staring at my mouth became "People looking at ME."

•*Drooling from the corner of my mouth became "I'll make handkerchief holders fashionable again!"*

I'm still working through the vanity aspect, and that's okay.

But my most serious fear was not being able to speak clearly. I make my living speaking, and this fear first came up during my initial surgery when a possible side effect was voice change.

I discovered that there are text-to-voice options, physical therapy, and even examples of speakers and comedians who have incorporated their "weaknesses" into their gigs with great success.

Facing my greatest fear freed me from its hold. It allowed me to go into surgery with a light heart and peace of mind.

Facing My Diagnosis: Fear of Death

When I was first diagnosed, I asked myself:

What's the worst that could happen?

The answer? Death.

And my biggest death-related fear? Not going to heaven because I no longer attend the church of my upbringing.

When I examined that fear further, I realized it was a holdover from my youth and not a belief I hold today. I am worthy of heaven!

With that realization, my mind was at peace.

Practical Steps for Peace of Mind

I also did practical things to bring peace of mind:

•*Updated my will*

•*Updated my Advance Health Directive*

•*Updated my business's emergency preparedness plan*

These tasks made my organized soul very happy. 😊

That's my process to feel at peace.

How do you find peace in difficult times?

How do you quiet your anxieties?

Please share your thoughts in the comments. Let's help each other find the best ways to stay centered and calm.

REFLECTIONS: FACING MY FEARS

When people ask me, "How did you stay so calm?" during my cancer diagnosis and treatment, I often joke:

"It wasn't my first rodeo."

But in truth, there were three key factors that helped me stay calm, grounded, and present throughout the experience.

I wouldn't say I never had moments of fear or doubt. I did.

But these three pillars made a huge difference in how I approached my diagnosis and navigated the journey ahead.

1. It Wasn't New to Me

One of the biggest reasons I was able to stay calm was that cancer wasn't new to me.

I'd already been part of the support teams for both my dad and sister during their cancer journeys.

I'd seen the behind-the-scenes realities of:

•Surgeries.

•Treatments.

•Doctor's visits.

•Recovery processes.

I knew what to expect — at least logistically.

The difference this time?

I was the patient.

It's one thing to support someone through cancer. It's another thing entirely to be the one lying on the operating table.

But even so, having that prior experience gave me a sense of familiarity that made the unknowns feel less scary.

I knew:

•The process.

•The language doctors used.

•What questions to ask.

And perhaps most importantly, I knew that:

People survive cancer.

2. Personal Development Work

I've been doing personal development work for years, and it turned out to be invaluable during this time.

One of the most impactful influences has been the work of Dr. John Demartini, whose teachings have helped me find balance and clarity in the midst of chaos.

His philosophy centers around the idea that everything has balance — even the hardest moments in life.

For every challenge, there's an opportunity.

For every pain, there's growth.

Whenever things started to feel overwhelming, I turned to his framework to help me reframe the situation.

Instead of spiraling into fear or "what ifs", I would ask myself:

•What's the lesson here?

•What's the opportunity in this challenge?

Here's the thing: fears don't go away by ignoring them. In fact, they often grow bigger when we try to push them aside.

What I've learned is that facing my fears head-on and figuring out what's at the core of those fears helps me feel more in control.

For example, when I found out I needed a neck dissection, I had some serious fears about the potential side effects. My biggest fear? A down-turned mouth — because let's be real, I'm a bit vain!

But when I really examined that fear, I realized it wasn't about looks. My core fear was losing my ability to speak clearly — something that's central to who I am and how I make a living.

Once I identified that core fear, I did what I always do: I looked for solutions. Knowing that I had options — like physical therapy and text-to-voice tools — gave me peace of mind.

I also leaned heavily on visualization techniques.

Every day, I would visualize my neck healing beautifully and without complications.

I would visualize my facial nerves returning to health, despite the major trauma they'd endured during surgery.

Remember, in my first surgery, the doctors had to peel my face back to expose the nerves and structures underneath.

The result? My face felt tingly and numb — a sensation that was disconcerting to say the least.

But instead of panicking, I visualized:

•Healing.

•Strength.

•Restoration.

It wasn't about denying reality. It was about creating a mindset of possibility and staying focused on positive outcomes.

3. Energy Healing with Caitlin McCoskey

The third pillar of my calm mindset came from an unexpected source: energy healing.

Now, I'll be honest — this was very "woo-woo" for me.

I'm naturally curious, but I'm also practical.

So, when a well-respected business coach recommended that I try a session with Caitlin McCoskey, an Energy Practitioner, I was skeptical.

But I also knew that I needed to strengthen my mindset as much as possible.

So, I booked a session.

And then another.

And another.

What Happened in Those Sessions?

I couldn't tell you how it works — and Caitlin made no grand claims about healing me.

But what I do know is this:

Every time I left a session, I felt:

•At peace.

•Reassured.

•Grounded.

It was as if her calm energy reached out to mine and left a little bit of itself behind.

There's a comfort in being with someone who exudes calm and kindness.

It reminded me that energy matters.

Who you surround yourself with — especially during difficult times — can have a profound impact on your mindset.

I had regular sessions with Caitlin from March to June, and each time, I left feeling more centered and better equipped to handle whatever was coming next.

KEY TAKEAWAYS FOR YOU

Here are a few things I've learned about staying calm during tough times that I hope will help you:

1. Draw on past experiences.

Even if you haven't faced this exact challenge before, you've overcome difficulties in the past.

What tools or lessons can you bring forward from those experiences?

2. Invest in your mindset.

Personal development work isn't just for good times. It's invaluable when life throws you a curveball.

Find frameworks and tools that help you reframe challenges and see the bigger picture.

3. Be open to new possibilities.

Whether it's energy healing, meditation, or something else, be open to trying new things.

Curiosity can open doors to unexpected sources of peace and strength.

4. Facing your fears is freeing.

Shine a light on your fears. The more light you shine on your fears, the smaller they get. When you face them head-on, they lose their power.

5. You always have options.

Even when things feel out of your control, there are always options to explore. Options bring peace.

6. Practical steps calm the mind.

When I updated my will, my Advance Health Directive, and my business's emergency plan, it wasn't because I was being morbid. It was because taking practical steps gave me peace of mind.

A PRACTICAL TAKEAWAY FOR YOU

If you're feeling overwhelmed or anxious, try this simple process to calm your mind:

1. Write down your fears.

Get them out of your head and onto paper. Even the silly ones!

2. Identify your core fear.

What's the biggest fear on your list? Dig deep — sometimes it's not what you think.

3. Make a list of past challenges.

What have you overcome before?

What tools or strategies did you use?

How can you adapt these strengths to help you face your fears you identified above?

4. Identify your calming practices.

Do you have visualizations, meditations, or affirmations that help you stay calm?

If not, start by visualizing positive outcomes for the situation you're in.

5. Explore new approaches.

Be open to trying something new, whether it's energy healing, breathwork, or mindfulness exercises.

6. Reframe your fears with humor.

I turned "drooling from the corner of my mouth" into "making handkerchief holders fashionable again." Laughter makes a huge difference.

7. Take practical steps.

Whether it's updating your will or simply organizing your thoughts, practical steps bring peace.

MOVING FORWARD WITH CALM AND CONFIDENCE

Staying calm through my cancer journey wasn't about denying reality or pretending everything was fine.

It was about:

•Drawing on past experiences.

•Using mindset tools I'd developed over the years.

•Being open to new approaches.

And perhaps most importantly, it was about reminding myself that:

"It's all good."

Because no matter what happens, there's always a way to find balance and peace.

CELEBRATING WITH THE CHICKENS — FINDING JOY IN UNEXPECTED PLACES

My Original Post

I MET with my ENT surgeons today and Loving Lumpy is confirmed as malignant and a super rare kind - primary squamous cell carcinoma.

The cancer was a 9mm section of one of the lymph nodes that runs through the salivary gland. The salivary gland was removed. All other nodes removed in my first surgery were clear of cancer.

My neck dissection is going ahead on Monday to remove four lymph nodes under my neck. Because there was cancer in that one lymph node, they want to be certain cancer hasn't travelled to other lymph nodes, as well as to prevent possible future travelling. There's not much research on my type of cancer given how rare it is so the docs are going with an abundance of caution.

Loving Lumpy is a wanted pathology specimen and I gave permission for it to be shared with other research centers. It's my prayer Loving Lumpy can help others!

Radiation will go ahead as soon as possible after this surgery. They don't like waiting long after tumor removal to do radiation and I've had a wait because of the second surgery. If I'd had both surgeries at the same time, I would have been starting radiation next week.

I also meet with two Physiotherapists to talk neck and shoulder exercises. There are a couple of complications that could arise from this upcoming surgery and the Physios have set me up for success with pre and post operative exercises.

Today was a day of firsts. The first time cancer had been definitively confirmed. The first time shown through the Oncology section as a patient. The first time with an Oncology Physio. The first time I've donated my tissue to medical research.

All of which made it a day to celebrate! A double sided hand towel in a chicken print caught my eye on the way out of the hospital and it's now found a new home with me. I couldn't think of a better way to celebrate a great day than with a chicken hand towel! (You'll see it in the video)

When I look back on this day, I see how important it is to celebrate milestones — even the ones that don't seem like traditional victories.

I walked out of that hospital with a sense of relief, gratitude, and joy. Sure, I still had another surgery and radiation ahead, but I had clear lymph nodes and a plan moving forward. That was more than enough reason to celebrate with a chicken hand towel!

REFLECTIONS: THE IMPORTANCE OF CELEBRATING WINS

When I think back to that first post-surgery hospital visit, I remember feeling a mix of emotions:

•Relief that I'd made it through surgery.

•Curiosity about what the doctors would say next.

•And a bit of nervous energy about the treatment plan ahead.

•It wasn't all good news, but there was enough progress to make me feel like I was moving forward.

But when the visit ended, I didn't feel worried or scared.

I felt calm.

And that, to me, was worth celebrating.

The Chicken Hand Towel

As I walked out of the hospital, I passed a little volunteer-run gift shop in the foyer.

It's the kind of shop that sells a bit of everything — books, gadgets, trinkets, and gifts.

I wasn't planning on buying anything, but as I glanced inside, something caught my eye.

A hand towel.

With chickens on it.

And I thought:

"Well, that's perfect."

Why Chickens?

I've always loved chickens.

During Covid, I had my own gaggle of backyard chickens, and they brought me so much joy and comfort.

Chickens are funny little creatures with big personalities.

They:

•Clean the soil.

•Announce the sunrise.

•And, of course, they give you eggs.

They're also low-maintenance pets, which makes them a great alternative for those who aren't ready for a dog (though I do love dogs best of all!)

When I saw that chicken-themed hand towel, it felt like fate.

Celebrating Milestones

I believe in celebrating milestones — whether they're big or small.

It's not about the size of the celebration.

It's about the deliberate intent of recognizing something important.

For me, that chicken hand towel became a symbol of a whole bunch of firsts from that day:

•First post-surgery hospital visit.

•First conversations about radiation and nerve damage.

•First time realizing I could handle difficult discussions calmly.

It wasn't just a towel.

It was a reminder that I had:

•Faced my fears.

•Had hard conversations.

•And done it all with grace and calm.

Finding Joy in Small Moments

That hand towel still makes me smile every time I see it.

It reminds me of:

•Strength.

•Calm.

•And the importance of finding joy in unexpected places.

Because life isn't just about big, grand moments.

It's about the little things that make us pause, smile, and say:

"I did that. I made it through."

KEY TAKEAWAYS FOR YOU

If you're navigating a challenging time, I encourage you to find small ways to celebrate your milestones.

Here's what I've learned:

1. Celebrate the little things.

You don't need a big party or an expensive gift to mark a milestone.

Even something as simple as a hand towel can become a powerful reminder of your strength and resilience.

2. Look for joy in unexpected places.

Sometimes, life's best moments come from unexpected finds — like a chicken towel in a hospital gift shop.

Be open to those moments, and embrace them.

3. Make your celebrations intentional.

It's not about the object itself.

It's about the meaning you attach to it and the story it holds.

4. Gratitude changes everything.

I've found that gratitude shifts my mindset from fear to hope. Being grateful for the progress I've made — no matter how small — helps me keep moving forward.

A PRACTICAL TAKEAWAY FOR YOU

If you're feeling stuck or overwhelmed, try this exercise to shift your mindset toward gratitude and celebration:

1. Write down three wins from your day.

They don't have to be big. Even small wins, like getting out of bed or making a phone call you've been putting off, are worth celebrating.

2. Find a quirky way to celebrate.

It could be a new coffee mug, a fun piece of clothing, or a treat you enjoy. Make it memorable and personal.

3. Share your win with someone.

Whether it's a friend, family member, or social media post, share your celebration. It spreads positivity and reminds others to celebrate their own progress.

MOVING FORWARD WITH JOY

That chicken hand towel wasn't something I went looking for.

But it turned out to be exactly what I needed to remind me of how far I'd come.

And if there's one thing I've learned from this journey, it's this:

Celebrate the milestones.

Even if it's just a towel with chickens on it.

Because joy can be found in the most unexpected places — if we're willing to look.

THE REALITY OF THE POSSIBLE
COMPLICATIONS HIT ME

*M*y Original Post

*THE REALITY of the possible complications for this surgery hit me today —
when I was enjoying a coffee at my local coffee shop. Not the best place to
burst into tears, but at least I was amongst friends.* 😄

*The doctor I saw during the week was new to me, and I describe him as a "bro
doc." All the arrogance and condescension from a time I thought was in the
past. I didn't realize until today how much I had allowed his attitude to
impact me.*

Note to self: Do a white light exercise if I'm ever near that doctor again.

*I spoke with my Anesthetist on Friday, who shared that my surgery will be
3½ hours. In my mind, that meant complicated, whereas I had thought it was
2 hours, so therefore, reasonably straightforward.*

*I find how our minds work fascinating. The same surgery, but with a
different timeframe, has rattled me. Nothing has changed with what the*

surgery is about — delicate and complicated skilled work. Only my perception of it.

I have also discovered that of all the possible side effects, it's the vanity one that bothers me — a turned-down mouth. It's never bothered me in others, but apparently it does for me. Side effects of a much more serious nature, like the possibility of losing full range of motion in my right shoulder, are something I'm happy to deal with if it happens.

For now, I'm allowing myself to feel the fear because I know I'll work my way through it to a resolution that sits well with me! Damn uncomfortable while in the process though! 😌

At the same time, I'm happy I'm in good hands and have everything going for me.

The tears were quite restorative, though. As was the hug from my barista, Ben! Thank you. 😊

REFLECTIONS: FACING THE REALITY OF COMPLICATIONS

When I reflect on this moment, I see how important it is to acknowledge our fears. Sometimes we don't even realize how much something is bothering us until it hits us unexpectedly — like it did for me in that coffee shop.

I've learned that it's okay to feel fear. What's more important is how we move through it. For me, it's about allowing myself to sit with those uncomfortable feelings, knowing that I'll come out the other side with a clearer perspective.

KEY TAKEAWAYS FOR YOU

Here's what I've taken from this experience that might be helpful for you:

1. Your perception matters.

Nothing about my surgery had changed, but my perception of it did. Recognizing that helped me take back control of my mindset.

2. Fear is a natural part of the process.

Feeling scared doesn't mean you're weak — it means you're human. The key is to let yourself feel the fear without letting it control you.

3. Seek comfort and connection.

That hug from my barista? It made a huge difference. Small moments of connection can be incredibly healing when you're feeling vulnerable.

A PRACTICAL TAKEAWAY FOR YOU

If you're struggling with fear or anxiety about something in your life, here's a simple process to help you shift your perception and move through those feelings:

1. Identify what's triggering your fear.

Is it a particular word, timeframe, or situation? Understanding the trigger can help you take back control.

2. Allow yourself to feel the fear.

Don't push it aside or ignore it. Sit with it for a while and acknowledge what you're feeling.

3. Reframe your perception.

Ask yourself: Has anything actually changed, or is it just my perception? Often, the situation hasn't changed — just how we're viewing it.

4. Seek comfort from someone you trust.

Whether it's a friend, family member, or even your local barista, connection is powerful. Don't underestimate the value of a kind word or a hug.

This experience reminded me that it's okay to cry in public — especially when you're surrounded by friends. Tears can be incredibly restorative and help clear the way for a calmer, more grounded perspective.

MARCH 27TH — FINDING COMFORT IN CONNECTIONS

y Original Post

I'M WAITING in the Admitting area and I'm feeling settled.

It was only as I was going through my admitting paperwork with the happy Linda that I twigged I had my first surgery on the 27th and now my second surgery on the 27th. I like synchronicity, so I'm going with this as a sign all is good! (Whatever it takes, right?!!) 😁

And then, as if to reinforce connections, I just saw two junior doctors from my previous visit, Kyle and Liam. Poor young Liam was the doctor who told me I had to stay an extra night last surgery (sorry about that, Liam! 😊 *).*

There's power in using people's names, and I always do my best to remember names. Calling these two guys by name brought a smile to their face in their busy day. That felt nice! 😌

Thank you everyone for your love 🤍 *I can certainly feel it* 🤍

REFLECTIONS: FINDING COMFORT IN CONNECTIONS

As I sat in the Admitting area waiting for my second surgery, I was surprised by how settled and calm I felt.

What stood out to me that day were the small connections that made me feel at ease — like noticing the synchronicity of both surgeries happening on the 27th, and recognizing familiar faces from my previous visit.

I've always believed there's power in using someone's name. It shows you see them as a person, not just a role. When I greeted Kyle and Liam by name, I saw how it brightened their day. Small moments of connection like that matter.

HOW DO I LOOK SO GOOD AFTER SURGERY

$\mathcal{M}$y Original Post

AS TO HOW I look so good after surgery, I was going to laugh it off and say, it's all filters.

Actually, it's the picture I carry of myself going into surgery. The only thing I can control is my feelings, so in the time leading up to surgery, I do what I call forward projection.

I focus on:

•How I'm going to feel going into surgery (relaxed, normal BP, laughing).

•How my team will be the best (I felt very reassured when I met them).

•How I'm going to feel when I wake up (alive, grateful, happy).

I cannot control whatever my new physical reality is, but I can control how I approach it.

That's not to say I'm not ecstatic that things are looking good so far!!! Hallelujah, sisters!

I hadn't quite worked it out in my head how I was going to deal with the possibility of a down-turned mouth, but I knew how I would feel to be awake and alive! And I dare say, some things can only be resolved if they become a reality.

So, for now, I'm feeling all the feels and grateful to be awake — although I'd really like to be asleep.

REFLECTIONS: THE POWER OF FORWARD PROJECTION

One of the most valuable tools I've used in my cancer journey is something I call forward projection. It's a way of visualizing positive outcomes and focusing on what I can control, rather than getting caught up in what I can't.

For me, that meant visualizing myself going into surgery feeling relaxed, calm, and happy.

It wasn't about pretending everything would be perfect. It was about setting the stage for how I wanted to show up emotionally, regardless of the outcome.

And let me tell you, it worked.

After my surgery, I got a lot of "You look amazing!" comments from people.

At first, I was tempted to laugh it off and say something like, "It's all filters," or "Thanks, it's the hospital lighting."

But deep down, I knew it wasn't about how I looked.

It was about how I felt.

I went into surgery feeling calm and prepared, and that inner peace reflected outward.

Plus, let's be honest — hospital gowns don't exactly scream glam.

Why Forward Projection Works

Forward projection is about taking control of your emotional state when life feels uncertain.

I couldn't control whether my surgery would be successful or whether I'd wake up with nerve damage or a down-turned mouth.

But I could control:

•How I felt going into surgery.

•How I approached the recovery process.

•How I handled whatever came next.

Gratitude and Humor as Coping Tools

One of the biggest lessons I've learned is that gratitude and humor go a long way in difficult situations.

Even when I felt exhausted or anxious, I made a point to find something to be grateful for — whether it was a kind nurse or just being awake.

And humor? Well, it's my go-to coping mechanism.

There were moments when I'd laugh at myself for the silliest things — like what I must look like walking around in a t-shirt, shorts, white knee-high compression socks, and sandals, or my "Something About Mary" hair.

FINAL THOUGHT: PROJECT YOURSELF FORWARD

I've found that projecting myself forward into challenging situations helps me stay calm and grounded.

It's not about pretending everything will be perfect. It's about choosing how you want to feel and show up, no matter what life throws your way.

And when all else fails?

Laugh.

Because life is unpredictable, and sometimes, a good chuckle is the best medicine.

POST SURGERY #2

⁂

M y Original Post

SURGERY WENT WELL, *and I have a new and beautiful scar to add to my collection* ❦ *I'm so lucky!*

The Consultant who did my first operation did this surgery too. It was reassuring to see him there. The other members of the team were new to me but friendly and loved a laugh. The Anesthetist wanted to know what I'd been doing to have resting BP and pulse. We had fun coming up with ideas!

Four lymph nodes were removed from my neck. Once again, the scar is a work of beauty!

Things took a bit longer because scarring from the first surgery got in their way. The doctor said the nodes looked good — not cancerous — but pathology will need to confirm that.

If the nodes are healthy, then YES!!!! That means radiation only on my parotid gland and none on my neck. Neck radiation carries a lot of risks, so no neck radiation would be the best next lot of news!

I'll know more in the morning when the team visits.

TRUE STORY

Anesthetic and the Art of Embarrassing Yourself

In case you didn't realize, anesthetic makes you relaxed — or, as my Anesthetist so kindly explained to me, "It will feel like you're drunk."

Which is great... until it isn't.

Because just like when you've had a few too many wines, your inhibitions drop, and whatever is front and center in your mind gets magnified.

And let's be honest — your social filter?

Gone.

Reunited with My Surgeon

For my second surgery, I was thrilled to learn that I'd been assigned the same surgeon I'd had for my first operation.

In the public hospital system in Australia, you don't get to choose your doctor. You get assigned a team, and you just hope for the best.

So, when I saw my original surgeon in the pre-op room, I thought:

"Perfect! He's already seen the inner workings of my face — we've been through this before!"

I figured he might even remember some of my internal quirks and little nuances from the first time around.

What I didn't expect was to make goo-goo eyes at him when he came to say hello before surgery.

The Mortifying Moment

There he was — my surgeon, standing by my bed to check in and give a quick "welcome back" before we headed into the operating room.

And there I was — full of anesthetic-induced relaxation, suddenly looking at him like he was the hero in a romance novel.

Goo-goo eyes, full force.

I was mortified.

The poor man made a hasty retreat, and I just wanted to sink into the bed and disappear.

Why Does This Happen?

I'm pretty sure it's not the first time a patient has acted that way, and I doubt it will be the last.

Let's be real:

When someone is potentially saving your life, it's not unusual to put them on a pedestal.

There's something about the power dynamic — your life is literally in their hands, and it makes sense that you might see them as a bit of a hero.

And in my case, it turns out that hero worship combined with anesthetic leads to a very awkward encounter.

I like to think he's probably seen it all before.

At least, that's what I tell myself to ease the embarrassment.

Embrace the Cringe

If I've learned anything from this experience, it's this:

Sometimes, life is awkward.

You'll have moments where you think, "Did I really just do that?"

And the answer is, "Yes. Yes, you did."

But you know what? It's okay.

In the grand scheme of things, a bit of awkwardness is a small price to pay for having a team of people working to keep you alive.

So, next time you find yourself embarrassing yourself in front of someone important, just remember:

We've all been there.

And chances are, they have too.

UPDATE MARCH 29TH

✦

*M*y Original Post

THE ONCOLOGY PHYSIOTHERAPIST *came to see me yesterday, and he reminded me of my lymphedema risks. That's another fun discussion no one ever wants to have — lol.*

I met with the Oncology Physiotherapists the week before surgery, and they gave me seven exercises to do to prevent lymphedema. This visit was to double-check that I was doing the exercises — I am! — and that I was nerve fit — I am!

It was a sobering visit, as it was a practical reminder that my life has changed. I will always need to be mindful of how my face and lymphatic system are draining.

I've enjoyed great health prior to this, and any surgeries I've had were what I call "start-and-end" surgeries. You go in, have your surgery to fix the problem, and that's it — problem solved.

Our chat was a reminder that my two recent surgeries are not start-and-end surgeries where I get to walk out the door and life continues on its merry way. These surgeries are only part of the process to living a long and happy life. They are not the end of the problem, like my other surgeries.

I have some lifestyle changes to incorporate into my life, and I'm quite intrigued as to what is to come.

I acknowledge that this particular post may come across as self-indulgent, and normally I wouldn't post something like this. But I have a feeling it may help someone, so here goes.

I'm a fan of serendipity and believe that clues are left throughout your life to help you in the moment you're in.

My decision to create this group and share what's going on came out of two seemingly unrelated conversations years apart.

My natural inclination when I found out I had cancer in December was to get on with treatment and keep it to myself. I'm not a big social media sharer, so it wouldn't have surprised anyone if I stayed quiet.

Then I remembered a conversation I had with a friend, Honey, who commented on my ability to quickly make connections between events and work through all the steps from A to Z in my mind at lightning-fast speed.

She pointed out that my superpower is that I see the big picture AND the details and have a very clear picture of what the end result looks like and how to get there.

The downside? I can fail to bring others along for the ride because they process information differently from me. They can't see the end result, or they need more information before fully committing.

The other significant conversation was with Caitlin, who encouraged me to share from my heart. She said that my open and honest communication about the cancer journey would help others.

In the work I do with my clients, I often talk about the importance of being authentic in their communication as they build their author brand and relationships with their readers.

How could I not do the same and show the same courage as my clients?!

And so, my hope with this group is to show you how I work through things and bring you along with me on this crazy ride.

Not because I have the answers or the right approach, but in the hope that an idea may spark for you and that you adapt something I share to work for you and your personality.

UPDATE MARCH 30TH

*M*y Original Post #1

BEING *in hospital is not for the weak of heart.*

Sigh.

Day 2 & 3 post-surgical sucks.

I'm not well enough to go home, but I'm not sick enough to be in hospital.

Throw in a roommate who plays their TV all night and another roommate who's on hourly observations, and it has me climbing the wall to get out.

I ended my night (or started my day) in the waiting room so I could get some rest.

I'm pretty sure that's not how things are meant to work, but hey, I'm adaptable.

Are we there yet?! Because I'm not enjoying this part of the journey.

MY ORIGINAL POST #2

Not quite how I was expecting my day to go, as I'll be staying in hospital rather than heading home. I'm giving the drain from my wound too good a workout, so I'm here until the bleeding comes under control.

It's been an interesting couple of days. I've decided that Day 2 & 3 post-surgical suck. It's like no-woman's land — I'm not well enough to go home, but I'm not sick enough to be in hospital.

I met with the Oncology Physiotherapists, and I have seven exercises to do to prevent lymphedema. There's another fun discussion no one ever wants to have — lol. However, I am nerve fit following surgery, which was great to hear!

It was a sobering visit as it was a practical reminder that my life has changed. I will always need to be mindful of how my face and lymphatic system are draining.

I've enjoyed great health prior to this, and any surgeries I've had were what I call "start-and-end" surgeries. You go in, have your surgery to fix the problem, and that's it — problem solved.

But my two recent surgeries are not start-and-end surgeries where I get to walk out the door and life continues on its merry way. These surgeries are only part of the process to living a long and happy life.

So, for today, I'll grow some patience and catch up on some sleep I missed, thanks to my roommate who had his TV on all night. Plus, there are those lifestyle changes to incorporate into my life — like the seven exercises — so I can go full steam ahead with whatever is next.

Highlight:

This morning, I had the full complement of doctors visit — not just the usual two familiar faces, but the whole team.

They were there to say, "Happy birthday!"

Now, let's be clear — their gift-giving skills? Terrible.

Apparently, their idea of a birthday present was making me stay longer in hospital.

But I've got to say, their cool factor went way up in my book!

Now, I'm not deluding myself.

I'm pretty sure the team wasn't gathered for birthday cake and celebrations.

This is a teaching hospital, after all. They had rounds to do, and I just happened to be the patient of the moment.

But here's the thing:

I've learned to reframe moments to suit me.

So, I'm choosing to see their visit as a serendipitous birthday surprise — and I'm sticking with that story!

After all, life's better when you add a little sparkle to the mundane moments, right?

Sometimes, you've got to create your own magic.

Reframe the unexpected moments in your life, and find the fun, even in a hospital room.

Because if there's one thing I know for sure:

It's all good. 😊

UPDATE MARCH 31ST

My Original Post

I'm in for another day 😄

The Docs have just been, and I'm in for another day.

As some of you may have twigged, there has been a snag with my recovery. My wound has been bleeding more than it should (three times more), and there were concerns I may have a slow bleed. The hope was that the bleed would stop on its own; otherwise, surgery would be needed to stop that pesky little sucker.

Fortunately, option 1 looks like it's the winner!

I find it challenging to be in hospital when I'm feeling well, and the boredom can make it an easy slide into losing perspective.

As Cheryl just reminded me when I whinged about being here another day, the news that my bleeding has slowed/settled means they don't have to go looking for a bleeder!

And that is fabulous news!

Perspective is everything! I lost perspective there for a bit.

One step at a time and stay in the step I'm in. 🌸

REFLECTIONS: EMBRACING THE PROCESS AND PATIENCE

This day reminded me that life doesn't always go as planned — but it's how we respond that matters.

I was expecting to go home that day, so being told I had to stay longer was a disappointment. But instead of letting frustration take over, I reminded myself that healing is a process.

There are moments in life when we find ourselves in "no-woman's land" — that uncomfortable space between where we were and where we want to be. It's not a fun place to be, but I've learned that patience and adaptability make all the difference.

KEY TAKEAWAYS FOR YOU

Here are a few things I've learned from this experience that I hope will resonate with you:

1. Healing takes time.

Whether it's physical, emotional, or mental healing, it's important to allow yourself the time and space to heal.

2. Patience is a skill worth cultivating.

I've learned that patience isn't just waiting — it's how we behave while we wait. Finding ways to stay calm and grounded during uncertain times is a valuable skill.

3. Lifestyle changes are part of the process.

I now have seven exercises to do regularly to prevent lymphedema.

It's a reminder that small, consistent actions can make a big difference over time.

A PRACTICAL TAKEAWAY FOR YOU

If you're feeling stuck in "no-woman's land", try this exercise to help you stay patient and present:

1. Acknowledge where you are.

It's okay to feel frustrated or impatient. Name what you're feeling and remind yourself that this phase is temporary.

2. Focus on what you can control.

There will always be things outside your control, but there are also things you can do right now to support your progress — like those seven exercises for me.

3. Practice patience.

Patience is a skill you can develop. Find small ways to practice it daily — whether it's waiting in line without checking your phone or sitting with uncomfortable feelings without rushing to fix them.

This experience reminded me that progress isn't always linear. It's about showing up, doing the work, and trusting the process — even when things don't go as planned.

UPDATE APRIL 1ST

❧

My Original Post

I'M free 🎈 🏡 No April Fool's for me!

Whilst my time was lovely and the care team were fabulous, I'm thrilled to be out of hospital. Thank you, Townsville University Hospital, for everything!

I'm tired, my neck is sore, and my throat and face are swollen, but that's all background noise to being at home (well, my brother's home in Townsville — but close enough).

Now it's time to actually get some sleep!

Next up: back to the docs for the pathology results on my lymph nodes and then radiation.

One step at a time!

REFLECTIONS: THE JOY OF FREEDOM AND NEXT STEPS

This moment was all about freedom and gratitude. After being in the hospital for longer than I'd hoped, getting out felt like such a win.

It's funny how even things like a sore neck and a swollen face feel insignificant when compared to the joy of being home.

What this experience reminded me is that gratitude and perspective go hand in hand. It's easy to get bogged down in discomfort or fatigue, but when I focused on the bigger picture — being free and out of hospital — it shifted everything.

KEY TAKEAWAYS FOR YOU

Here are a few things I've learned from this experience that I hope might help you:

1. Celebrate your freedom.

Getting out of a challenging situation — whether it's the hospital or something else — is always worth celebrating. Don't take freedom for granted.

2. Gratitude shifts your mindset.

Even when you're tired and sore, focusing on what you're grateful for can change your whole perspective.

3. One step at a time.

It's easy to get overwhelmed by what's next, but I've learned that focusing on one step at a time makes everything feel more manageable.

A PRACTICAL TAKEAWAY FOR YOU

If you're feeling overwhelmed or stuck in a challenging situation, try this exercise to shift your mindset toward gratitude and freedom:

1. Identify a recent win.

What's something you've recently accomplished or overcome? Acknowledge it and celebrate it, no matter how small it might seem.

2. Focus on the present.

Instead of worrying about everything ahead, ask yourself: What's the next step? Focus on one thing at a time.

3. Find something to be grateful for.

Even if you're tired or uncomfortable, there's always something to be thankful for. Gratitude can change your whole outlook.

This moment reminded me that freedom is a gift and that taking life one step at a time makes even the toughest journeys more manageable.

UPDATE APRIL 11TH - CLEAR LYMPH NODES AND A FUTURE BELL RINGING!

y Original Post

HIGHLIGHTS:

•My lymph nodes are clear of cancer 🦷

•Radiation will be only on my parotid area ☢️

I went to many medical meetings today — think ENT surgeons, ENT radiation oncologists, oncology physiotherapist, oncology speech pathologist, social worker, and oncology dentist — to get the results of my lymph node extraction and map out the next steps in my treatment.

The ENT surgeons are very happy with my healing. My lymph nodes have come back all clear, which is fabulous news! My wound is a thing of beauty, and I have minimal side effects from the two surgeries (though I do have a decrease in taste buds doing their thing).

My Oncology team are thrilled with my speed of recovery and believe I'll be a good candidate for four weeks of radiation at a higher dose (five days a week), rather than six weeks at a low dose. There are pros and cons to both options, but four weeks is right for me, and I'm happy to get it done and get on with healing!

Because my lymph nodes were clear of cancer, radiation will only be on my parotid area — no radiation on my neck! I'm beyond thrilled by this.

My fitting for my full head mask — think Jason horror movie style — is next week, with radiation starting not long after that.

I've never had radiation before, so it's another new experience coming up. What I do know is that at the end, I get to ring the bell! I was there when Cheryl got to do this following her breast cancer radiation, so I'm all prepped for this part! Let's ring that bell!!!

The oncology dentist was delighted to tell me that my teeth are in great condition, which makes me dentally fit for radiation. In another moment of serendipity, the dental work I had done last year in preparation for my total knee surgery has meant that I'm good to go for this treatment.

A side effect of radiation is that any teeth extractions will now need to be done by a specialist. This is because my jawbone is unlikely to close on its own after an extraction due to the effects of radiation. This is true for life.

Of all the things I learnt today, that was the most sobering. I'm not planning on having any teeth removed, but I'm going to have to visit my dentist every three months for life to ensure all is well.

The recurring message today was that I'm healing really well, and my prognosis is good.

Oh, and I've trained my ENT surgeons well! I greeted each one by name this morning, except for a new junior doctor. Two of my long-term doctors turned to her and said, "It's best you introduce yourself because Narelle likes names." We all laughed, and I got to meet Lucy, who was slightly bemused by me.

And one more thing — Dr. Gemma did the stitching of both my wounds, and her sewing skills are superb. I shared with her (and the team) that she ruined my plans to be a pirate because of her exquisite stitching. She was thrilled! It was important to me that she know how grateful I am for her expertise and care. 🎈

REFLECTIONS: CELEBRATING PROGRESS AND EMBRACING NEW EXPERIENCES

It was a big day of medical meetings, and by the end of it, my brain felt like it had done a marathon. ENT surgeons, radiation oncologists, speech pathologists, social workers, physiotherapists, dentists — you name it, I saw them!

But here's the best part:

•My lymph nodes were clear of cancer! 🩺

•Radiation will only be on my parotid area. ☢

Those two pieces of news made everything else feel a little easier to handle.

Serendipity and Celebrating Progress

I noticed serendipity popping up again during this visit.

First, I realized that both of my surgeries had happened on the 27th of the month. I'm not saying that's a magical number, but I like finding little connections like that. It makes me feel like things are falling into place.

Then, I learned that the dental work I'd had done last year in preparation for my total knee surgery meant that I was already dentally fit for radiation. It was like past me had unknowingly prepared future me for this moment.

It's moments like these that remind me to trust the process — even when life feels uncertain.

The Radiation Mask Fitting: Jason Vibes!

Next up is my radiation mask fitting, which is an experience in itself.

If you've never seen a radiation mask, just picture something out of a Jason horror movie — a full head mask that gets molded to your face to keep you still during treatment.

It sounds a bit terrifying, but for me, it's just another new experience to navigate. And at the end of it?

I get to ring the bell! 🔔

I was there when Cheryl rang the bell after her breast cancer radiation, and I've been waiting for my turn. There's something about that simple act of ringing the bell that symbolizes victory and progress. I'm ready for that moment!

Doctors, Names, and Pirate Dreams

One thing I've noticed is that using people's names makes a huge difference in how they respond to you.

When I greeted my ENT surgeons by name, two of them turned to the new junior doctor and said, "It's best you introduce yourself because Narelle likes names."

We all laughed, and I got to meet Lucy, who seemed a bit bemused by me. But hey, she knows my name now! ☺

And then there's Dr. Gemma, who did the stitching for both my surgeries. Her sewing skills are so perfect that I had to tease her:

"You've ruined my plans to be a pirate with that exquisite stitching!"

She was thrilled to hear that her work was appreciated. And it was important to me that she knew how grateful I was for her expertise and care.

REFLECTIONS: CELEBRATING PROGRESS AND EMBRACING NEW EXPERIENCES

This update was full of good news and moments of serendipity that reminded me how everything is connected.

Hearing that my lymph nodes were clear, and that radiation would only be on my parotid area felt like a huge step forward in my journey.

I've learned that progress looks different for everyone. For me, it's about celebrating each milestone, no matter how small, and embracing new experiences — even when they're a bit scary (like the radiation mask fitting).

A PLAYFUL TAKEAWAY: MAKE YOUR OWN BELL-RINGING MOMENT

Life may not always come with a literal bell to ring, but that doesn't mean you can't celebrate your victories.

Find your own way to mark progress — whether it's a toast with friends, a happy dance, or even a new chicken towel! (You know I love those!)

Because every step forward — no matter how small — is worth celebrating.

UPDATE APRIL 18TH — THE MASK, THE PLAN, AND A TANTRUM IN THE MAKING

❦

*M*y Original Post

WELL, today was probably the lowest day I've had so far over the last four months. I had my radiation planning session for the mask I will wear at every session, and I met my oncology care team to go over how to look after myself during my treatments.

Once again, I'm blown away by how fabulous everyone is. There is love and care in their actions, which is heartwarming. 🤍

My Oncologist told me my treatment plan has changed — instead of four weeks and just my parotid, I will now be having radiation on my neck as well as my parotid, and treatment will be five days a week for six weeks. Bah humbug! I so did not want to adult at that point. A nice four-year-old's tantrum would have been just the thing!

The reason for the change: Research has shown there's a 30% chance of SCC cancer appearing in lymph nodes if left unirradiated, even if nodes were clear. As much as the treatment plan change rattled me, I know the docs want to give me the best chance of a full recovery. I'll happily trade an extra two weeks of radiation for a long and happy life!

Having my mask fitting was freaky-ass weird! Laying down on the CT table, I was placed in guides so I couldn't move — vital when taking pinpoint calculations with the CT.

The doctor marked on me where he wants to radiate, and wire was placed along my scars and against the parotid. Then the Radiation Techs formed the mask around my face and shoulders using breathable moldable plastic.

The mesh plastic (thermoplastic) sheet they use for the mask is softened in hot water. The sheet is then placed over your face and shoulders and molded to your face and body, and secured to the table. It takes about 10 minutes for the material to harden. During that time, you lay still, with your eyes and mouth closed, breathing normally.

The plastic is breathable, so you don't have breathing tubes in your nose. Let me tell you, the plastic feels like a wet slimy creature has attached itself to your face! I had to remind myself I could breathe because my mind was telling me I couldn't since both my mouth and nose were covered. The sensa- tion was freaky! And it's quite the head spin!!!

Once the mask was hard, it was bolted to the table to hold me in position so I couldn't move (you can see the nine black bolts in the pic below). Using lasers, they calibrated the CT to my mask and the spots and wire they physically put on me. This was all then programmed into the machine. So, when treatment starts, they call up my program, and away we go.

Following that little mind muck, the Oncology RN, Cat, took me through the personal do's and don'ts and what to watch out for. Suffice to say, I want none of what she was sharing! 😬

I will find out next week when radiation starts, and it will be nice to have a little bit of certainty back.

My most important job now? Naming my mask. Something this green and good-looking needs a cool name! Any ideas???

REFLECTIONS: FACING UNCERTAINTY AND FINDING HUMOR

I'll be honest — this day shook me.

Up until this point, I had been riding a wave of optimism, buoyed by good news and small victories. But hearing that my treatment plan had changed, and I'd need six weeks of radiation instead of four?

That was a punch to the gut.

I didn't want to adult in that moment. I wanted to stomp my feet, throw my hands up, and let out a loud "NOPE!"

But life doesn't work that way, does it?

The truth is, there was no negotiating with cancer. The doctors made it clear that this new plan was the best way to ensure that my treatment would be as effective as possible.

So, I did what I've learned to do:

I took a deep breath, accepted the change, and looked for a way to bring humor into the moment.

Getting Fitted For My Mask

This was the hardest thing I have ever experienced. I came so close to a panic attack so many times during this fitting. Even knowing breathing techniques and mind work, I was literally saying to myself, "Just continue for five more seconds. OK, now another five seconds. And now another five seconds."

I knew if I did not complete the mask creation, that I would have to do it again or go without radiation. The only thing greater than my fear in that moment was my fear of dying because I did not kill all the cancer. Having my face encased in a solid membrane without breathing holes was like a top five ways not to die list come true. The membrane is breathable so I could continue to breathe but because there were no visible breathing holes (to me), my mind just lost it.

121

Naming My Mask: Why Humor Matters

Naming my mask? That was my way of taking back control. It reminded me that even when I don't get to choose what happens, I can still choose how I approach it.

And trust me — finding a bit of humor in a situation that feels utterly terrifying makes all the difference.

I've always believed in naming things to make them less scary. It's why I named my tumor "Lumpy" — because once it had a name, it became something I could talk about without fear.

The radiation mask was no different.

When I was laying on that CT table, with a wet, slimy sheet being molded to my face and shoulders, it felt like I was in a scene from Alien or Jason from Friday the 13th. 🎥 🔪

But the moment I decided it needed a name, it shifted from being a terrifying piece of medical equipment to being less scary and something I could do.

That mask wasn't just a symbol of radiation treatment — it became something I owned.

Finding Humor in Hard Times

One thing I've learned on this journey is that humor doesn't take away from the seriousness of what you're going through.

It's not about pretending everything is fine.

It's about acknowledging that things are hard — and finding a way to bring lightness into the darkness.

For me, it was naming the mask. For you, it might be making a joke, wearing a silly T-shirt, or even watching a funny movie.

Humor helps us cope. It reminds us that we're still human — still alive — even in the hardest moments.

In my terror of the mask creation, I realized,

- The next six weeks would be tough. Radiation five days a week is no walk in the park.
- My mindset needed a top-up because I needed to be able to wear that mask, bolted down to the table, for 5 minutes a session, for 30 sessions.
- I'm stronger than I think. And when it's all over, I'll be ringing that bell with everything I've got.

A FINAL THOUGHT: FINDING LIGHT IN THE DARK

If you're navigating your own hard time, I hope this reminds you that it's okay to feel rattled. It's okay to have moments when you want to throw a tantrum.

Just don't stay there.

Find something light — a joke, a name, a moment of connection — and let it help you move forward.

Because even when life feels uncertain, we have the power to bring light and humor into it.

UPDATE MAY 8TH — START OF RADIATION WITH PERCY PARROT BY MY SIDE

*M*y Original Post

RADIATION ✦ STARTED TODAY, *and I got to wear my freshly minted green warrior queen mask.*

Putting my mask on today was actually comforting. It's a very close fit, and I certainly could not move, but it fit my face perfectly and felt more like an embrace than a restrictive mask. Knowing that I can easily wear the mask at each treatment has removed my concerns about a claustrophobia freak-out.

The setup takes longer than the treatment, which is only 3 minutes long.

During treatment, I'm required to stay very still, and they give you a rectangle object for both hands to hold over your stomach. It keeps your upper body and arms in the right position whilst, I dare say, also helping relieve tension.

Back when I first found out I was having surgery and that I'd have a good-sized scar, I joked about being a pirate. Aaargh! My dear friend Crystal's kids made me an eye patch and a parrot — essentials for any self-respecting pirate!

Well, I never got to dress up as a pirate because my scar was so well blended, but I could think of no better way to take the world-wide love flowing to me into my treatments than to swap out the generic hospital rectangle with Percy Parrot. 🦜 Percy P. did a fabulous job today!

My mantra continues to be "It's all good" ... because it is! As the lights flashed and the machine whirred around me, my meditation was, "Cancer out, abundance in!"

I'm so incredibly grateful as I continue to see the weaving of providence in all that's going on.

My radiation team today were Kim and Aaron, with the wonderfully welcoming Sandy on front desk. Afterwards, Vanessa, the oncology nurse, gave me a spot quiz on my do's and don'ts. I got a C grade. 😊 Apparently, "That's on a sheet at home" is not the right answer lol.

The biggest don't? Don't lose weight. It has a significant impact as I'd need a new mask created and a new radiation plan created.

It's likely that all food will taste like cardboard, and my mouth and throat will be inflamed, so eating enough to maintain my weight is my focus.

Vanessa's best advice for keeping weight on??? Drink McDonald's thick shakes. Easy on the throat and full of weight loss preventers. 😋

So, my radiation journey begins. For the next six weeks, Monday - Friday, I'll be getting zapped.

Cancer out, abundance in!

As a side note, my patience muscle is no more developed than before Loving Lumpy arrived. Patience needs to work on her timeliness because she sucks at it.

REFLECTIONS: FINDING COMFORT IN THE UNEXPECTED AND THE POWER OF PERCY PARROT

Radiation treatment is a daunting word, isn't it? It sounds clinical, serious, and a little bit scary. I'll admit, I felt nervous about starting this phase of my treatment. The idea of being strapped down by a custom-fitted mask for six weeks of daily radiation? Not exactly a highlight on anyone's to-do list.

But what surprised me most was how quickly I found comfort in the unexpected.

The green radiation mask — which initially seemed intimidating — felt more like a protective shield when I wore it. It fit perfectly, molded to my face like a gentle embrace. What had once been a source of apprehension became a source of comfort.

And then there was Percy Parrot.

Let me tell you about Percy. He wasn't just any parrot. He was crafted with love by my dear friend Crystal's kids after they heard me joke about becoming a pirate with my scar. Complete with an eye patch and a colorful fabric body, Percy was the perfect pirate accessory.

But more than that, Percy became my companion in every radiation session.

Instead of holding the standard hospital prop, I held Percy — a tangible reminder of the worldwide love and support that was with me during treatment.

When I lay there with my mask bolted to the table and the radiation machine whirring around me, Percy reminded me that I wasn't alone. He was a symbol of connection, of love and lightness in a situation that could easily feel overwhelming.

The Magic of Bringing Something Personal Into the Process

There's something powerful about making a medical process personal.

For me, it was swapping out the generic rectangle object for Percy Parrot. It made the experience feel less clinical and more human.

Every time I gripped Percy's fabric body, I remembered the laughter and love that went into making him. He grounded me in those moments when I could have easily spiraled into anxiety or fear.

Radiation wasn't just about destroying cancer cells — it became about embracing life and finding joy in the process.

Why Humor and Joy Matter, Even in Serious Situations

One of the best lessons I've learned from this journey is that humor doesn't take away from the seriousness of what's happening. It's not about pretending everything is okay when it's not.

Instead, it's about choosing to find lightness — even in moments that feel dark.

Percy Parrot wasn't just a funny addition. He was a beacon of joy. He reminded me that even in the face of something as serious as cancer treatment, I could still laugh, connect, and find comfort.

And I'll take joy and humor over fear any day.

KEY TAKEAWAYS FOR YOU

Here are a few things I've learned from this experience that I hope might resonate with you:

1. Make it personal.

Find a way to bring something meaningful to you into challenging situations. It might be a mantra, an object, or even a playlist of your favorite songs.

2. Humor helps you cope.

A little laughter goes a long way. It doesn't minimize the seriousness of what's happening — it just makes it easier to handle.

3. Connections matter.

Whether it's a physical object like Percy Parrot or a text from a friend, those moments of connection remind us that we're never truly alone.

A PRACTICAL TAKEAWAY FOR YOU: BRING A BIT OF JOY INTO TOUGH TIMES

If you're facing a challenging experience, here's a simple exercise to help you find lightness and comfort:

1. Find a personal token of comfort.

It could be a stuffed animal, a piece of jewelry, or even a lucky charm. Choose something that makes you feel grounded and connected.

2. Incorporate humor into the experience.

Can you give something a funny name? Your medication, your treatment schedule, or even your mask? Laughter helps soften the edges of difficult moments.

3. Focus on who's with you in spirit.

Even if you're physically alone, remember the people who care about you. Whether it's a text, a call, or even a parrot named Percy, those connections are powerful.

A FINAL THOUGHT: CANCER OUT, ABUNDANCE IN

During each radiation session, my mantra was, "Cancer out. Abundance in."

It was a reminder that while cancer may be part of my story, it doesn't define it. There's so much more to life than illness — and by focusing on gratitude, connection, and joy, I was choosing to bring abundance into my life.

And let's be honest — Percy Parrot stole the show.

Because sometimes, all you need to face a tough day in a green mask, is a quirky parrot, and a little bit of laughter.

UPDATE MAY 10TH

*M*y Original Post

HERE'S some action shots from Day #3 of radiation:

•Photo 1: You can see the green lines on my face, showing that I'm in the right position on the bed.

•Photo 2: Once the mask is secured into place, the placement lines on the mask match up to the green lines, ensuring my face, mask, and machine are in sync.

•Photo 3: As you can see, the mask is a close fit.

Percy, the photo hog, is in pics 2 & 3! 🐦🦅

The treatment takes 3 minutes with the round bit with the blue light sweeping across both sides of my face and neck several times.

Today was my third session, and I've mastered getting my head in the right position for the mask — slightly tilted back.

During treatment, the team plays the music of my choice, which is mostly Aussie Pub Rock — John Farnham, Jimmy Barnes, B-52s, The Angels (not that song though! 😄), Crowded House, and so on.

I also saw my Oncologist Dr and my Oncology Physio today, and both are happy with my progress.

Go me 🌷

"It's all good! Cancer out. Abundance in."

UPDATE MAY 12TH

❦

*M*y Original Post

I THOUGHT *I had nailed my mindset and settled in well to my radiation treatments. Oh, how wrong I was. Day 5 of treatment had me struggling not to panic. This was full on terror taking over my whole body.*

I became restless and my heart rate went high. I wanted out of that mask, and I was going to rip it from the table if I needed to. Nothing I could do seemed to be working, from breathing to affirmations to cursing my reason for being there.

Stopping the treatment and removing the mask saved the day. The technicians knew something was up from the monitors (and my body language) and gave me a moment mid-treatment to regroup. I was able to breathe through my terror and do a reset to allow me to lie back down and start the treatment again.

The terror shut my brain down and I could feel my heart squeezing and staying tight. I was full on scared.

The treatment is over, and I have the weekend to recalibrate and how much do I need that. I was scared but was able to complete the treatment. However, I left my session scared that my usual coping strategies were not working and I have five more weeks of treatments.

Cancer sucks!

REFLECTIONS: THE PANIC AND THE MANTRA

I still remember the exact moment I realized I was about to lose it during this treatment. My mask was clipped into place in nine places, and I could feel my heart pounding in my chest. My brain was yelling at me to rip the mask off and run. It was full-on terror.

I couldn't move. I couldn't run. So, I turned inward.

I repeated my mantra over and over: "Cancer out, abundance in." But nothing. The terror was greater than anything I had in my arsenal in that moment.

Having the opportunity to get out of the mask and catch my breath was a godsend. I knew I had to do the treatment, so I went through my affirmations and deep breathing exercises. At first, it felt mechanical — like I was just going through the motions. But slowly, my body started to calm down. I reminded myself that this was a step toward healing. I reminded myself that I was in control of my mind, even if my body felt out of control.

That mantra became my lifeline during those tough moments. It was a reminder that I could get through it, one breath at a time.

The remembered terror is not so powerful these days, but I have not forgotten it.

WEEK 1 RADIATION WRAP-UP — THE HIGHS, THE LOWS, AND PERCY PARROT

$\sim\!\!\infty\!\!\sim$

*M*y Original Post

I DISCOVERED a few things during the first week of radiation, and I wanted to share them with you in case it helps you.

My care team continues to reinforce that I need to maintain my current weight during my six weeks of radiation. What a blessing this has been!

As someone who's been overweight most of my adult life, suddenly switching my focus from losing weight to being healthy has been, well, healthy.

I've found myself making smarter choices with a focus on health rather than listening to all the negative self-talk I carry around weight. This is one lesson that's staying with me.

I've been asked about my focus on taking names and using them, wanting to know what that's all about. 😄

I find all things Medicine to be scientific, cold, and clinical. It's a bit like a conveyor belt, and I understand the need for that because our community's health needs are many.

However, I needed to make my surgery and treatment personal, and the best way I know to do that is to form a personal connection with my amazing team. And the best way I know to connect with a new friend is to use their name... and so I do.

The other part of remembering everyone's name is that it forces me to be present. By focusing on remembering each person in my care team, my mind cannot drift to other things because it's busy building neural pathways linking faces and names.

I have a bit of facial blindness where I don't always recognize faces. I've learned tactics over the years to link faces and names, but it remains a struggle at times. Being present is my most effective tactic.

Week 2 starts in just a couple of hours, and I'm having not only radiation today but also meeting with the Oncology Nurse.

Being the Type A I am, I boned up on the myriads of info I've been given to make sure I've been doing what I was told. It's a bit like taking a test!

Hopefully, I'll get a passing grade.

Have a great week, everyone! Thank you for your support!

REFLECTIONS: SHIFTING FOCUS AND BUILDING CONNECTIONS

This week highlighted three powerful themes: changing my mindset around health, the importance of personal connection, and that progress is not linear.

Shifting my focus from weight loss to staying healthy has been a game-changer. Instead of listening to negative self-talk, I'm making healthier choices out of self-care rather than punishment. That's a big mental shift.

Taking names and building personal connections has helped me stay present during treatment. Using someone's name makes the process less clinical and more human.

Some days, you'll feel like you're on top of the world. Other days, you'll feel like the world is on top of you.

Both are valid. Both are part of the journey.

What matters is that you keep showing up, even on the days when it feels impossible.

And when the terror hits, it's okay to pause. It's okay to take a moment to breathe, reset, and try again.

KEY TAKEAWAYS FOR YOU

Here are a few things I've learned from this experience that might help you, too:

1. Focus on health, not weight.

Shifting my focus from losing weight to staying healthy has been empowering. It's about making smart choices that support my well-being.

2. It's okay to feel fear.

Fear is a natural response to difficult situations. Acknowledge it, but don't let it control you.

3. Progress is not linear.

There will be ups and downs. Celebrate the good days and give yourself grace on the hard ones.

A PRACTICAL TAKEAWAY FOR YOU

If you're navigating a health journey or stressful environment, try these steps to shift your mindset and build connections:

1. Focus on making healthy choices.

Instead of thinking about what you want to lose, focus on what you want to gain — like energy, strength, or peace of mind.

2. Be gentle with yourself when your reptile brain takes over.

We are human and there are times when we feel like we have failed to live according to our principles. It is ok. You are ok.

3. Give yourself permission to pause.

If you're overwhelmed, it's okay to pause and regroup. You're not giving up — you're giving yourself a moment to breathe.

This week taught me that small mindset shifts can have a big impact. And that sometimes my reptile takes over.

FINAL THOUGHT: IT'S OKAY TO BE SCARED

If there's one thing I've learned from Week 1 of radiation, it's this:

It's okay to be scared.

What matters is that you keep going anyway.

And if you need a little help along the way, bring your Percy Parrot — or whatever reminds you that you're not alone in this journey.

Because we're never truly alone. Even in the darkest moments, there's always someone or something that brings us light and love.

Cancer out, abundance in!

UPDATE MAY 16TH

❧

*M*y Original Post

I'M OVER IT. I don't know how people with long-term pain or ongoing conditions do it.

I'm six sessions in and ready to stop.

My days are not my own. I get notice on a Friday of my appointments for the following week, so Friday feels like a scramble to rework my upcoming work week to fit the hospital's schedule.

I hate that mask. It feels super restrictive this week, and I just want it off.

I knew I would get to this point because it's part of human psychology, but I thought it would kick in around the week 4 mark, not the start of week 2.

REFLECTIONS: HITTING A WALL AND PUSHING THROUGH

This was a tough moment. It felt like hitting a wall. I knew this point would come — where everything feels overwhelming and I'd want to stop — but I wasn't expecting it so soon.

What I've learned is that it's okay to feel frustrated. It's okay to not be okay for a moment. The important part is recognizing it and finding a way to push through.

I also realized that being adaptable — adjusting my schedule each week based on hospital appointments — is challenging but necessary.

This phase of my journey reminded me that progress isn't always linear. There will be days when it feels harder than expected, but that's part of the process.

IT'S NOT A PRETTY REFLECTION

The other thing that stood out for rereading this post is the lack of gratitude for exceptional medical care. In the moment, I lost focus on gratitude and the focus was on me and my schedule. I feel embarrassed to include this post because it shows how selfish I was, but it is more important to me that I show my total experience, not just the good parts.

HOW TO HELP A LOW-MAINTENANCE FRIEND

⚜

My Original Post

WHEN A FRIEND'S *life is turned upside down, we tend to jump into help mode. "How can I help?" "What can I do to help?"*

But what do you do when your friend is low maintenance?

I had never considered this question until my cancer diagnosis. I was always the "helper" to others and was pretty good at it. I'm also a task-focused personality, so doing things for others was well within my wheelhouse.

Then I got cancer, and suddenly I had friends and family asking me how they could help and support me.

I'm a low-maintenance sort of woman. I'm organized, I have a strong sense of self, and I've been up close and personal with cancer before, with both my dad and sister. I knew the ropes.

For My Fellow Low-Maintenance Friends:

It doesn't matter how often you say you're okay, some will think you're faking it and tell you it's okay to ask for support. Let it flow off your back. Focus on the love that person has for you and how abundant you are because of their love.

Being low-maintenance can be confronting for others who aren't that way or are used to dealing with high-maintenance friends, family, and situations. They don't know what to do with you!

Make it easy for your friends and family and share with them how you want to be supported. I started a Facebook group to share my cancer journey because I wanted connection with friends around the world, a place where they could pop in, say hello, and find out how things were going.

What you don't want to do is close yourself off to others. For me, being open was through a Facebook group. You may use a different tool, but at the core, you need to have a place to connect.

I also recognize it's hard for friends of low-maintenance people not to feel like they're speaking in platitudes because there's nothing much else for them to do. When words are all you can offer, it's hard to come up with new ways of saying, "I'm in your corner."

Your job is to make it easy for your family and friends. Instead of words, write a post and ask for responses with their best emoji or gif.

For the Friends of Low-Maintenance People:

Firstly, know you're loved by your low-maintenance friend.

Understand that your friend will let you know when action is needed. Until then, just be around like usual. Resist the urge to ask how they are. Instead, share a funny post or gif, share about your life, and chat like you usually would.

Believe your friend when she says she's okay and on top of things.

Be ready when she asks for help — because she will ask when she needs it.

REFLECTIONS: NAVIGATING SUPPORT FOR LOW-MAINTENANCE FRIENDS

Before cancer, my natural way of processing things was to figure it out in my head. I've always been independent, capable, and practical — I'd sort through my thoughts quietly, make a plan, and get on with it. But here's the thing: when you do that, people around you have no idea what's going on inside. They see you've moved from A to Z, but they have no idea how you got there. It leaves them unsure if you need help, and when people are unsure, they usually don't act.

That's something cancer made me rethink.

After my diagnosis, I realized that people need a combination of emotional and practical support. I received a lot of practical help from my brother and sister-in-law while I stayed with them during radiation. Having a place to stay was huge — it took a big weight off my shoulders. But what I also appreciated were the casual emotional check-ins. Nothing heavy or dramatic, just a "How are you doing?" over a cup of tea or a quick chat after dinner. That combination of practical help and emotional connection was heartwarming.

But I knew I needed to be proactive about asking for help. So, I made two conscious decisions:

1. I would write about my cancer journey in my Facebook group to keep people informed and connected.

2. I would actually ask for help — even if I wasn't sure I needed it. You can never have too many laughs, after all.

My Facebook group was incredible. Whenever I needed cheering up, I'd ask for memes and funny videos, and they delivered in spades. I remember one day feeling a bit low, so I asked for a laugh, and within hours, my group was filled with hilarious posts. It was such a simple way to lift my spirits and feel connected to people who cared.

Story: The Surprise of Asking for Less Help Than People Expect

What I found interesting, though, was that other people's perceptions of cancer were different from my experience. I was expecting this massive life upheaval, but for me, things weren't as bad as I'd feared — certainly not as bad as what my dad and sister went through. I was able to continue with life fairly normally.

I thought I was asking for help when I needed it, but I soon realized that wasn't what other people expected. There's this belief that all cancer patients need a lot of help, and some of my friends and family were worried that I wasn't asking for more help.

I remember one conversation where a friend said, "Are you sure you're okay? You can ask for anything, you know."

I laughed and said, "Honestly, if I needed more help, you'd be the first to know. But right now, I'm good."

Their response? "Well, we're ready to drop everything if you need us."

It was such a kind sentiment, but it also made me realize that people associate cancer with constant need. In reality, it depends on the person and their situation. For me, I appreciated knowing that help was there if I needed it, but I didn't want people to feel like they had to be on call 24/7.

KEY TAKEAWAYS FOR YOU

Here are some things I've learned from this experience that might resonate with you:

1. Don't assume people know what you need.

Even if you're independent, people around you may not know whether you need help. Communicate clearly — it removes the guesswork.

143

2. Ask for help, even if you're unsure.

Sometimes we hesitate to ask because we think we don't want to bother anyone. But people want to help. Giving them the opportunity to do so is a gift.

3. Perceptions of need vary.

Your experience may not match other people's expectations. That's okay. Let them know how you're really doing and what kind of support you actually need.

A PRACTICAL TAKEAWAY FOR YOU

If you struggle with asking for help, here's a simple exercise to make it easier:

1. Make a list of things people could do to help.

These don't have to be big things — it could be sending a funny meme, dropping off a meal, or taking your dog for a walk.

2. Communicate your needs clearly.

Let your friends and family know what kind of support feels right for you. This could be through a group message, an email, or even a quick chat.

3. Give people permission to check in.

If you don't always know what you need, let people know it's okay to reach out. Sometimes, just knowing someone is there makes all the difference.

MOVING FORWARD: SHIFTING HOW WE VIEW SUPPORT

This chapter made me realize that support isn't a one-size-fits-all approach. We each have different needs, and that's okay. The key is clear communication and staying connected in ways that feel right for you.

And if you're ever unsure how to help someone, remember this: A roast chicken, a kind word, or even a funny gif can go a long way in making someone feel loved and supported.

Cheers to that!

SUPPORT NETWORK

My Original Post

THANK you to everyone for being here for me. I'm blest with an international circle of friends and family who cover me in love 24/7. I am one lucky woman. 🤍

PRACTICAL SUPPORT — IT'S NOT ALWAYS ABOUT THE WORDS

I have to be honest:

I'm one of those people who doesn't always know what to say when someone shares bad news with me.

In the past, I'd often find myself staring at a blank card or drafting a message, struggling to come up with something meaningful to say.

So, I created a swipe file — a collection of phrases and responses I'd seen that resonated with me.

Now, I keep that swipe file handy so I don't have to reinvent the wheel every time I want to offer support.

Having those ready-to-go responses takes the pressure off and allows me to focus on showing up rather than worrying about finding the right words.

Sometimes Actions Speak Louder Than Words

What I've also learned is that you don't always need words to offer support.

During my dad's illness, one of the most meaningful acts of kindness came from Rhonda, who dropped off a roast chicken at our house every second Friday.

It wasn't just about the food.

It meant:

•I didn't have to think about cooking.

•The chicken often lasted two meals.

•And it was one less thing to worry about during an emotionally exhausting time.

At work, someone anonymously left me a flower every week.

I never found out who it was, but I didn't need to.

I love flowers, and the simple gesture of receiving one flower each week was deeply meaningful.

These acts of kindness and thoughtfulness reminded me that support comes in many forms.

Being Real — It's Okay to Say, "That Sucks"

In the past, I used to focus on saying the "right" polite words.

Now?

I focus on being authentic.

When someone shares difficult news with me, I'm more likely to say:

•"Damn! That wasn't part of the plan!"

•Or "That sucks."

It may not sound poetic, but it's real, and it comes from the heart.

I've found that people connect more deeply with honest, heartfelt responses than with polite platitudes.

Shining a Light on Dark Topics

One of the biggest shifts I've experienced since my cancer journey is my willingness to talk openly about difficult topics — including mortality, fear, and grief.

In the past, I might have avoided those conversations.

Now, I believe in shining a light on the things that scare us.

Of course, I always ask the other person's permission first.

Something as simple as:

•"Would you like to talk about what you're feeling?"

•Or "I'm okay if you want to talk about the hard stuff."

Often, there's a sense of relief when I offer to go there.

People want to talk about these "dark" topics, but many are afraid to bring them up.

I'm not afraid anymore.

I've learned that talking about mortality, fears, and grief doesn't make those things more real or more powerful.

If anything, it reduces their power.

REFLECTIONS FOR YOU

If you're unsure how to offer support to someone going through a difficult time, here are some reflections to consider:

1. Practical help can be more valuable than words.

•Bring a meal.

•Send a small gift.

•Leave a flower.

•Sometimes, actions speak louder than any words you could say.

2. Create a swipe file of responses.

•If you struggle to find the right words, start building a collection of phrases that feel authentic to you.

•Ask ChatGPT (a conversational AI chatbot) for suggestions, or jot down responses you see and like.

•Having a swipe file will make you feel more prepared to reach out when someone needs support.

3. Don't be afraid to go to the "dark" places.

•If someone needs to talk about mortality, fear, or grief, ask for permission to explore those topics with them.

•You don't have to fix their feelings — just be present and hold space for them.

A PRACTICAL TAKEAWAY FOR YOU

If you want to strengthen your ability to offer meaningful support, here's a simple exercise to try:

1. Create your own swipe file.

•Think of five phrases you'd like to say when someone shares difficult news with you.

•Save them in a notes app or journal.

2. Think of a practical way to show support.

•Could you drop off a meal?

•Send a small gift?

•Or do something as simple as leaving a flower on their desk?

3. Practice being real.

•Next time someone shares bad news, try responding with something authentic, like:

•"That sucks."

•"Damn! That wasn't part of the plan!"

See how it feels to be honest and real.

MOVING FORWARD WITH AUTHENTICITY

A support network isn't just about being there when someone needs you.

It's about knowing how you want others to show up for you — and practicing those same behaviors when it's your turn to offer support.

Be real.

Be present.

And don't be afraid to go to the places others won't.

Because sometimes, all it takes to make someone feel loved and supported is a store-bought meal or a simple flower.

UPDATE MAY 22ND WEEK 3

$$\mathcal{C\!S}$$

*M*y Original Post

I'M a third of the way through my radiation treatments and starting Week 3 today! Only four more weeks to go!

I had a rocky start to Week 2 when I was a hair's breadth from having a panic attack on the previous Friday (week 1) and then again last Monday (week 2). When the final two bolts were clipped in last Monday, my crocodile brain nearly took control. It was only my mantra that kept me on the table.

I was also super ticked off last Monday. The best word to describe my mood was resentful. I was resentful that my body had betrayed me. That my time was being taken up with radiation. That I was the patient, and not the visitor.

I meet with the Oncology Nurse every Monday after treatment, and we laughed and laughed about me needing to wear a hat even in the car! I know right! Only old Italian men do that! (In Ayr (my home town) anyways.) Laughter truly was the balm for my soul that day and reset my perspective.

I am forever grateful I've spent time strengthening my mindset over the past two decades because I needed every ounce of that experience last Monday.

If you're not already doing mindset work, don't put it off a minute longer. There are all sorts of benefits to nurturing a strong and resilient mind, not the least of which is if you should find yourself with a health challenge.

Tuesday through Friday passed without issues — probably because Hugo the Trainee was there, and his earnestness was such a delight.

Over the weekend, I had a few things kick in:

•Food now tastes like cardboard.

•My mouth is always dry and tastes like a dirty sock.

•The right side of my throat is swollen.

•My right ear has swelled to almost closed.

My trusty medical team had prepared me for these things and have given me great suggestions for how to adapt to them so that I keep eating. Which of course means I've moved to soft foods.

I did test the boundaries on Sunday night by eating Vegemite on toast, and whilst the salty Vegemite taste was divine (radiation is no match for my Vegemite taste buds 😋), my throat did not appreciate me. So, I've taken Vegemite toast off the menu for now.

But, all in all, I'm doing great.

I'm continuing to work. I went to Bjorn Again and sang and danced the night away to ABBA. Life doesn't get better than that!

Here's to a happy Week 3! 😄

It's all good!

REFLECTIONS: NAVIGATING EMOTIONAL SWINGS AND
FINDING JOY

Week 3 of radiation treatments felt like a turning point for me. By that point, I had settled into the routine of treatment, but I also hit some emotional bumps that caught me off guard.

One of the biggest moments was the panic I felt on that Friday of Week 1 and Monday of Week 2. I remember lying there as they clipped the final bolts on my mask (there were 9 in total), and suddenly my crocodile brain — the part of our brain responsible for survival instincts — decided it was done. My body was screaming, "Get out!" and I had to use every ounce of mental strength to stay on that table.

What saved me that day was my mantra: "Cancer out, abundance in." It gave me something to focus on other than my rising panic. That moment taught me that even the strongest mindset can be tested, and it's okay to feel overwhelmed. What matters is finding a way to reset.

The other big emotion that hit me in Week 2 was resentment. I hadn't anticipated feeling that way. I was resentful of my body for betraying me, resentful of the time and energy being taken up by treatments, and resentful of the fact that I was the patient instead of the visitor.

But then something amazing happened. I had my check-in with my Oncology Nurse, and we laughed and laughed about me having to wear a hat even in the car to protect my skin from the sun. That laughter was the reset I needed. It reminded me that I could find lightness even in heavy situations.

And then there was Hugo the Trainee. His earnestness and eagerness to do a good job were so endearing that it lifted my spirits every time I saw him. There's something about seeing someone new to their role, full of enthusiasm and care, that's incredibly heartwarming.

Even with the physical side effects kicking in — like the dry mouth, swollen throat, and cardboard-tasting food — I found moments of joy.

I still went to see Bjorn Again and sang and danced to ABBA songs all night. That night reminded me that life doesn't stop just because you're going through treatment. There's always room for joy if you make space for it.

The Joy of ABBA

Going to see Bjorn Again during treatment felt a bit rebellious. I mean, I was in the middle of radiation, dealing with swollen throats and dry mouths, but I wasn't going to let that stop me from having fun.

When the music started, something shifted in me. I forgot about cancer. I forgot about treatments. I was just there — singing, dancing, and soaking up the joy of the moment.

The best part? I wasn't alone. I was surrounded by people who were there to have a good time, too. It reminded me that joy is contagious. When we embrace those moments of lightness, we spread it to those around us.

And let's be real — who can resist singing along to Dancing Queen?

KEY TAKEAWAYS FOR YOU

Here are a few lessons I've learned from this experience that might resonate with you:

1. Mindset work pays off when it matters most.

It's easy to dismiss mindset work as fluff when things are going well. But when things get tough, that work becomes your lifeline. It's worth the time and effort to build a strong mental foundation.

2. Laughter is a powerful reset button.

Even in the darkest moments, there's room for laughter. It doesn't take away from the seriousness of what you're going through — it just gives you a moment to breathe and reset.

3. Joy is a form of resistance.

When life feels heavy, finding moments of joy is an act of rebellion. It's a way of saying, "I'm still here, and I'm still living."

A PRACTICAL TAKEAWAY FOR YOU

If you're navigating a long-term challenge, here are some steps to help you manage emotional swings and find moments of joy:

1. Create a mantra.

Find a phrase that feels meaningful to you and use it as a grounding tool during tough moments. Repeat it to yourself when you need to stay calm or focused.

2. Seek out humor and laughter.

Watch a funny movie, share a joke with a friend, or find something to laugh about. It's a simple way to lift your spirits.

3. Make space for joy.

Even if it's something small — like dancing to your favorite song or savoring a treat you love — make time for moments that bring you joy. It's those moments that help balance out the tough times.

MOVING FORWARD: FINDING BALANCE IN THE HIGHS AND LOWS

This chapter reminded me that life is a series of highs and lows. There will be moments of terror and moments of joy, and both are part of the journey.

The key is to find balance. Acknowledge the tough moments, but don't forget to seek out the lightness, too. Because even in the hardest times, there's always room for joy, laughter, and connection.

And let's not forget: It's all good.

MOST CHILLED PATIENT

My Original Post

My Radiation Therapist gave me the biggest compliment today, "you're always our most chilled patient".

REFLECTION:

Just looking at this post makes me smile. It was a good day!

RADIATION PLAN

❦

My Original Post

THIS IS MY RADIATION PLAN...

Imagine you are standing behind me and able to look through the back of my head through to my face. The two white circles at the top are my eye sockets.

Down towards the middle of the image, the two vertical white bits are the top of my jaw. The small white bottle shape towards the bottom middle is the start of my spinal cord.

Now come down the right side, and you'll see a multi-colored area. This is where all the action is taking place!

The intensity scale of the radiation dose I'm getting is:

•Red (highest radiation dose)

•Pink

•Blue

•*Green*

•*Yellow (weakest dose)*

The directly targeted site is encased in a red line. You'll see the parotid is getting the strongest dose of rays (red/pink/yellow/green) with the surrounding area, neck, and lymph nodes getting a reduced dose (pink & aqua blue).

It's no wonder my neck is a lovely shade of red!

The extended darker blue that goes out over my mouth and nose defines the area that does not get any targeted zapping but does get some leakage.

Isn't tech amazing that they can focus and morph the radiation on such an odd-shaped area!!!

Kim and Aaron were so excited to step me through my plan. They're fabulous professionals, and I'm grateful for their skill and dedication.

REFLECTIONS: GRATITUDE FOR SCIENCE, EXPERTISE, AND VISUALIZATION

Seeing my radiation plan brought a surprising sense of comfort and empowerment. It wasn't just a clinical image to me — it became part of my mental and emotional process during treatment.

Kim and Aaron were thrilled to walk me through the plan, and their enthusiasm was contagious. They clearly love their work, and I could tell they don't often get the chance to share their expertise in such detail. Knowing they were excited to explain things made me feel seen and cared for. It also reminded me how passionate people can be about their jobs, even in high-pressure fields like oncology.

Learning what the different colors meant, how the machine worked, and understanding that radiation is delivered at specific points in the machine's cycle helped me relax during treatments. I realized I had it all wrong before! Knowing when the radiation was being delivered — and what all the sounds and movements of the machine meant —

made a huge difference. It took away the unknown and turned it into a process I could follow along with in my mind.

The visual plan also helped me picture my affirmation more clearly. As I lay on the table and said, "Cancer out. Abundance in," I could visualize the radiation precisely targeting the cancerous areas. It wasn't abstract — I could see it in my mind.

It also made me more mindful of how to care for my body. Seeing where the radiation would hit — and where the overflow would go — helped me focus on protecting those areas. I covered them up better in the sun, rubbed them with lotion, and spoke kindly to them, thanking them for doing a great job holding strong against the radiation.

Radiation is an incredible tool, but it has side effects. The technology today makes it more precise and reduces risks to healthy tissue, but there's still overflow into surrounding areas. Understanding that made me appreciate my care team's precision and feel more proactive about my own care.

KEY TAKEAWAYS FOR YOU

Here are some insights from this experience that I hope you'll find helpful:

1. Understanding your treatment can reduce anxiety.

Taking the time to learn what's happening to your body — and why — can help make the process less scary and more empowering.

2. Turn treatment into a mental exercise.

Pairing visualizations or affirmations with your treatment can make you feel more engaged and in control.

3. Care for the whole body.

It's not just the target area that needs care. Pay attention to the surrounding areas as well and give them love and attention.

A PRACTICAL TAKEAWAY FOR YOU

If you're facing a medical treatment or complex process, here are a few steps to help you feel more comfortable and in control:

1. Ask questions.

Don't be afraid to ask your care team to explain your treatment plan in detail. Most professionals love sharing their expertise.

2. Pair your treatment with affirmations.

During treatments, use a positive mantra to focus your mind. Visualize the process as it happens to stay grounded.

3. Show gratitude to your body.

Thank your body for its strength and resilience. Care for areas affected by treatment, even if they aren't the direct target.

MOVING FORWARD

This experience taught me that understanding the process and making it personal can transform something intimidating into something empowering. Radiation treatments weren't something I feared anymore — they became a process I actively participated in. And that made all the difference.

NO TASTE BUDS

*M*y Original Post

No Taste Buds

I've hit the three-week mark in my radiation (putting me halfway through my treatment plan) 🍽️ , and my taste buds have officially gone on strike.

This was expected and has been kicking in and out this past week — but it's still quite a shock to the system!

I'm home in Ayr for the weekend, and I just had a world-famous Phelan's pastie. Nothing. Zip. Nada. 😣 That makes it official.

My brother says I now have two taste descriptors:

• Tastes like poison (chocolate & coffee)

• Tastes like cardboard (everything else)

It is temporary, and this too shall pass.

It's all good 😄 *(except the coffee part. That's bad! Just saying!* 😅 *)*

REFLECTIONS:

Cancer sucks!... and taste buds are super important!

UPDATE MAY 29TH — STAYING IN THE STEP YOU'RE IN

y Original Post

I MET *with the Oncology RN yesterday.*

I've lost 0.4kg (0.8 pounds) since last week. The max I can lose is 1kg (1.6 pounds) before they get really nervous. That's how tight the mask needs to be!

From memory, a 4kg loss is the danger mark, and I'm a ways from that, so I assume any weight loss has my medical team jumping on it as prevention is better.

I tried McDonald's shake, but I didn't tolerate that well. I'm going to buy cream today because that's been ok so far, and it's high calories. I'll put it on my rolled oats in the morning.

The irony is my face and throat are swelling due to the treatments, so the mask is tight! But my shoulders need to stay the same shape.

UPDATE MAY 30TH

My Original Post - Week 4 Wrap-Up

Week 4 has been a mixed one. Monday and Tuesday were great, and then I felt like I slipped down a great big slippery slope without any catch holds into meh land.

I had a really bad zap on Wednesday. I was a hair's breadth away from fighting the mask and crying. I haven't felt like that since Friday of Week 1.

My neck is so swollen from the build-up of lymph fluid that the mask is super tight. My eyelashes were pressed up against the mask, and it freaked me out. I like to have my eyes open during treatment as it lessens the claustrophobia, but now I'm closing my eyes and doubling down on my mantra.

You do whatever you need to do to get through!

After the treatment, the Radiation Therapist came in and asked if I was struggling at the start as my stats were elevated. She also said they could see me bring it down and stabilize.

My mindset has been the glue that's held me together over the last six months. But to be honest, I'd had enough on Wednesday, and I wanted to tap out — even though I know that's not an option.

Thursday's zap went much better, and I have just one more to go before Week 4 is done!

Up until this stage, I've handled things pretty well, but something about Wednesday set me off. I don't know what — just a general sense of unease. Maybe thinking that if we'd stuck with the original plan of four weeks of radiation, I'd be done. And so, wanting to be done now!!!

It doesn't help that my wattle allergy has kicked in! (At least I hope it's allergies and not a cold.) There's a huge wattle tree out the front of Kevin's place, and it's blooming its little heart out.

I had slept poorly on Tuesday night because I couldn't breathe when I lay down. Allergy tablets and a puffer have started to kick in now, though.

As I was buying food for the week, I also caught myself thinking, "There's no sense buying good quality food. I can't taste it."

Now, more than ever, I need healthy food, but I'm just not interested in eating. This active disinterest in food only kicked in on Tuesday.

I mean, honestly, how much weight can I lose in two weeks that's going to make a difference to my mask?!

I know if all things were usual, I wouldn't drop enough weight to make a difference in two weeks, but I dare say that mischievous imp will have me dropping weight like nothing else now that things are not usual. A pox on him!

And it turns out, I have lost weight. I saw the dietitian on Thursday, and I've lost a kilo in one week. That's a red flag. ▶

Food I am eating includes:

•Avocado on toast

•Rice pudding

•Egg custard

•Scrambled eggs

Not surprisingly, they are comfort foods from my childhood. I'm crumbling goat's cheese on the avocado and eggs for added goodness.

I also have stews that are semi-whizzed up. Oh, and rolled oats for breakfast, now with cream.

Strawberries are also good with a dash of cream.

That's about it, though. I truly could never eat again right now, although I live in eternal hope my taste buds return because I miss food.

The reality is that I've lost a salivary gland, so it's possible my taste buds will never be the same, and dry mouth will be something I need to learn to live with.

It can take up to six months for my new normal to be apparent after radiation, so I have a little while yet before I know what 'normal' looks like for me.

It feels like a good time for me to recommit to placing one step in front of the other and staying in the step I'm in.

It's all good 🤍

So, if you find yourself accepting less than the best anywhere in your life, know you are worthy of healthy choices, just like I am.

REFLECTIONS: THE ROCKY ROAD OF WEEK 4

There's something about being halfway through a long-term challenge that brings up unexpected emotions. I started the week in a good place, but by Wednesday, I found myself slipping down a mental slippery slope.

I had a bad zap that day. My neck was so swollen from the buildup of lymph fluid that my mask was painfully tight. My eyelashes pressed against the mask, which freaked me out more than I expected. I like to keep my eyes open during treatment to manage any feelings of claustrophobia, but with my eyes forced shut, I felt trapped.

The Radiation Therapist noticed something was off. After my treatment, she told me my stats were elevated at the start but that she saw me bring them back down and stabilize. That's what mindset work does for you — it doesn't prevent you from feeling fear or frustration, but it gives you the tools to manage them.

Still, I was tired. Tired of the routine. Tired of the mask. Tired of the treatments.

I hit a wall of resentment, thinking, If we had stuck to the original plan of four weeks of radiation, I'd be done now.

But life rarely goes to plan, does it?

Taste Buds on Strike and Comfort Foods

One of the toughest parts of Week 4 has been the loss of taste. Food tastes like cardboard, my mouth is always dry, and swallowing is uncomfortable.

My Oncology Nurse and Dietitian have been fantastic, reminding me how important it is to maintain my weight. The challenge? Eating when you're actively disinterested in food.

The foods I am eating — rice pudding, scrambled eggs, stews, and avocado on toast — are comfort foods from my childhood. Funny how, when things get tough, we gravitate toward what feels familiar and comforting.

And let's talk about the irony of my situation for a moment: My face and neck are swollen, but my shoulders need to stay the same shape for the mask to fit correctly. Meanwhile, I'm losing weight despite eating cream and custard. The goal is to keep my weight steady so I don't need a new mask and treatment plan.

The Emotional Roller Coaster

By Wednesday, I was over it. Completely over it.

I wanted to tap out.

But I knew I couldn't.

So, I reminded myself to stay in the step I'm in.

It's a phrase I've leaned on heavily during this journey. It means focusing on the moment you're in rather than getting overwhelmed by the entire journey ahead.

It doesn't make the hard moments go away, but it helps you take one step at a time — and sometimes, that's all you need to do.

Percy Parrot: A Feathered Reminder of Support

During this tough week, Percy Parrot came with me to every treatment. Crystal and her kids sent me Percy, a soft cloth parrot, as a symbol of their love and support. Holding Percy during treatments was like holding their hands — a comforting presence that reminded me I wasn't alone.

And isn't that what support is all about? Finding ways to show up for each other, even from a distance.

KEY TAKEAWAYS FOR YOU

Here are some lessons from this experience that I hope might help you:

1. Stay in the step you're in.

When life feels overwhelming, focus on the present moment. It's all you need to manage right now.

2. Find comfort in the familiar.

Whether it's a favorite childhood food or a symbol of support like Percy Parrot, find something that grounds and comforts you.

3. Mindset work matters.

Your mindset won't prevent challenges, but it will help you navigate them.

A PRACTICAL TAKEAWAY FOR YOU

If you're feeling overwhelmed by a long-term challenge, try this exercise to help you stay grounded:

1. Acknowledge your feelings.

It's okay to feel frustrated or tired. Name what you're feeling without judgment.

2. Focus on one step at a time.

Instead of worrying about the whole journey, focus on the next step in front of you.

3. Find a comforting reminder.

Whether it's a favorite food, a comforting object, or a supportive friend, find something that reminds you, you're not alone.

MOVING FORWARD: STAYING PRESENT AND FINDING JOY

Week 4 reminded me that progress isn't always linear. There will be highs and lows, and that's okay.

What matters is how you respond to those lows.

For me, it was about reconnecting with my mantra, leaning on my support system, and focusing on one step at a time.

And, of course, holding on to Percy Parrot — my faithful feathered friend who brings a little bit of joy to every treatment.

Because even in the hardest moments, there's always room for joy.

UPDATE JUNE 2ND- SNOT HAPPENS

~~~

*M*y Original Post

I JUST HAD my last zap for Week 4, and I ended on a memorable note!!!!

Anyone easily grossed out may wish to skip this update. It's funny but gross!

I have an allergy-induced nose cold, and my nose is pretty blocked. Imagine the worst thing that could happen while you have a nose cold and you're bolted to the bed by a fine mesh mask?!

You guessed it!!! I sneezed in my mask mid-treatment.

I elected to continue going rather than start again. The worst had happened, and there was every chance it could happen again, so I'd rather get the treatment over and done with.

I have now finished Week 4, and I have one more thing crossed off my never-do-again list! 😄 😝

You couldn't make this stuff up! I'm all good 😄 *It's absolutely hilarious.* 😄 *You can just call me, Snotty McSnotFace.* 😝

170

In case you're concerned:

The team were wonderful, and we had already discussed my options in situations like this, so I knew I could keep going or stop, clean up and start again.

It was my decision to continue. The team kept checking in with me and were incredibly kind and responsive after. As they said, they've seen it all. 🩶

REFLECTIONS: WHEN LIFE HANDS YOU SNEEZY MOMENTS

Sometimes, the hardest moments turn into the funniest stories — at least, in hindsight!

Sneezing into my radiation mask wasn't just gross; it was a moment that could have derailed my treatment. But once it happened, I realized that I could either laugh or let it ruin my day. I chose laughter.

It also made me appreciate the empathy and care from my radiation team. They knew how unsettling a moment like that could be, and their compassion made a huge difference.

My radiation team had discussed with me prior to treatment about how we could handle things if I sneezed into my mask. Option 1 was to keep going and clean up after the treatment was done. Option 2 was to stop the treatment, clean up, and then start the treatment again.

I chose option 1 and I would make the same choice today. I just wanted the treatment done.

This experience reinforced a valuable lesson: unexpected things will happen, and you can't control them. But you can control how you respond.

Choosing laughter helped me stay grounded and get through the rest of my treatment. Plus, it gave me a new nickname: Snotty McSnotFace. 😊

KEY TAKEAWAYS FOR YOU

1. Humor is a powerful coping tool.

Even in serious situations, finding something to laugh about can help you stay grounded.

2. Compassion makes a difference.

The kindness of others can help turn a challenging moment into a manageable one.

3. Embrace the unexpected.

Things won't always go as planned, but how you respond is within your control.

A PRACTICAL TAKEAWAY FOR YOU

If you're facing an unexpected or awkward moment, try this exercise to help you find humor and stay grounded:

1. Acknowledge what happened.

Name the situation and how it made you feel. It's okay to feel embarrassed, scared, or frustrated.

2. Look for the humor.

Ask yourself: What's funny about this moment? Even if it's something silly or gross, humor can help lighten the emotional load.

3. Accept kindness from others.

Let those around you offer support, whether it's a kind word, a smile, or a joke.

MOVING FORWARD: EMBRACING LIFE'S AWKWARD MOMENTS

Sneezing into my radiation mask wasn't on my to-do list, but it became a memorable (and hilarious) moment in my journey.

Life will throw awkward, unexpected moments at you, and sometimes, they'll be downright gross. But choosing laughter and accepting kindness from others can turn those moments into stories that make you smile later on.

Here's to embracing life's sneezy moments — and finding joy in the unexpected.

And remember, you can always call me Snotty McSnotFace.

UPDATE JUNE 3RD — WHEN LIFE TASTES LIKE TIN

*B*efore I share this update, I want to explain why I'm letting it stand on its own.

This wasn't one of those moments where I sat back, reflected, and came up with brilliant life lessons. Nope. This was a "just get through the day" kind of moment. I wasn't looking for takeaways or philosophical insights. I was wandering my kitchen, hoping food would stop tasting like dirty socks soaked in tin.

And that's the point.

Sometimes, you're not interested in being enlightened or becoming a better person. You're just trying to find something — anything — that doesn't taste like roadkill. You're holding on for the bubbles in a Coke, hoping they'll bring a spark of life back to your taste buds. You're navigating moments when resilience isn't pretty or polished.

So, I'm leaving this post exactly as I wrote it at the time. Because in that moment, there wasn't anything more to say.

MY ORIGINAL POST

Here's what I discovered at the end of Week 4.

My initial broad view of treatment truly became reduced down to the minute.

How could I get through this meal? What could I eat that would taste nice? (Hint: nothing).

I was hungry and hunting for food while at the same time wanting nothing to do with food.

The metallic taste in my mouth is indescribable. I explained it to the dietitian, nurses, and doctor as "tasting like poison" even though I've never tasted poison.

The inside of my mouth was like a combination of:

•Dirty socks

•A month of unbrushed teeth

•Poison

•Tin

•Roadkill baking in the hot Australian sun

I'm doing a lousy job of describing what the inside of my mouth feels like, but think of the worst possible taste for you and then multiply it by one hundred.

The more focused I became on the minutiae, the greater the negative impact on my mental health. It took several days to notice what was going on, and once I did, I was able to shift my pattern.

For me, that's humor.

Laughter lightens my load and makes my day happy. During this particular week (Week 4), it was laughing with my dietitian that set me to rights.

The right person or situation has always shown up when I've needed a laugh.

So, don't worry about looking for someone. Instead, be open to experiencing laughter, and the right person or situation will show up.

I was not prepared for my biggest struggle to be around my crappy taste buds.

The treatments are quick and painless.

The persistent tin taste in my mouth is abhorrent.

It's currently taking me an hour to eat each meal.

Everything that has come before this is nothing compared to the trauma that is eating.

I roam the kitchen and pantry looking for food that will take away this horrible tin taste in my mouth.

I think I've tried everything in the hope that something brings me flavor, but nothing works — except Coke.

Coke tastes tinny, but not as much as everything else.

Its redeeming feature is the bubbles.

The bubbles are a lifeline.

UPDATE JUNE 4TH

It's funny how life's hardest moments don't always call for grand wisdom or motivational quotes. Sometimes, what we need most is a good laugh. At this point in my journey, I knew I was entering the toughest stretch — physically, mentally, and emotionally. I was scared, and I knew the weeks ahead were going to test me in ways I hadn't yet experienced.

But rather than asking for inspiration or advice, I asked for something simpler. I asked for laughter. Because when life feels unbearable, sometimes a good meme or a dad joke is the best medicine of all.

MY ORIGINAL POST

Ok folks, there's a change in the rules!

It looks like things are progressing nicely for me into burnt skin, sores, mouth ulcers, and all-around ouch, so I'm changing up the rules.

I think everything else that's gone before will be nothing compared to this next stretch.

I'm slightly scared I can't do this next stage even though I know I have to. I even know the reality of what's coming! I've supported my sister and dad through this stage, and I know what's ahead. I've dressed their wounds and cried with them as they struggled with the pain.

I hope I can weather this next part as well as they did!

The effects of radiation compound over time, which means they'll keep working for two to four weeks after treatment ends.

I have two weeks of treatment to go, plus two weeks of compounded reaction time.

So, I just want to warn you that you may be confronted by what I'm going to look like over these next four weeks.

I don't know how things are going to go, but I do know that laughter is my key for thriving.

It's weird, isn't it?! When you think this is the situation where inspirational words would be most vital, they are, in effect, the least needed.

So, please, hold back with the inspirational messages. 🩶

Instead, you can best support me over this next intense period by making me laugh.

Dark humor. Gallows humor. Humor humor. Dad joke humor.

I don't mind. Share your wicked sense of humor with me in memes, GIFs, and short videos.

The best way to support me is to help me laugh!

UPDATE JUNE 5TH—THE POWER OF ONE SMALL FIX

*In any tough journey, there are moments when the smallest of breakthroughs can feel monumental. For me, that moment came when I discovered Mucosoothe. After weeks of struggling with the metallic taste in my mouth, this thick, syrupy solution didn't just numb the pain — it brought me back to life in a way.

Sometimes, it's not about a grand solution or a complete turnaround. It's about finding one small fix that changes everything.

MY ORIGINAL POST

What a Difference a Day Makes!

Firstly, can I just say you all rock!!! Thank you so much for all the funnies you shared as soon as I asked for help.

Humor is my glue, and at the lowest point in this crazy trip, you guys delivered exactly what I needed to lift me out of despair and sadness. I can't say thank you enough!!!

Week 5 started on Sunday with a blast... literally.

Everything was on fire in my mouth 🔥 *The burns we had been expecting showed up on Sunday, with my neck and face now a lovely bright red along with darker spots on my neck.*

Thankfully, my external burns are not painful or itchy, and for that, I give thanks daily. 😄 *I know how lucky I am to be pain-free in Week 5!*

But the inside of my mouth and neck is on fire with rashes and sores. If I thought eating was unappetizing before, it became even worse over the weekend. I stopped eating because I couldn't stomach food that tasted like poison, even though I kept my two liters of water up!

Well, wow! What a difference 24 hours makes!

Monday's zap went super well. Super quick and easy with my favorite Radiation Therapists on the job.

Mondays are also Oncology Nurse days, and those appointments are always a hoot.

Today, though, things were different. Nurse Bency was on the job and brought in the Registrar to help me with my burning mouth and throat.

Turns out I have thrush on my tongue, which is exacerbating all the other things going on in my mouth. As soon as the doc said thrush, I thought, "That's right. Ok, things are looking up!"

The nurse seemed surprised by my positive reaction, but I explained that I remembered Dad had thrush with his radiation, too, and that this was something we can fix.

The doc prescribed Mucosoothe, a super thick anesthetic syrup that I swill around my mouth and swallow to numb everything for 15 minutes.

The clever doc got me to try it by saying it removes the metallic poison flavor from food, which got my attention. I don't mind pain, but the loss of taste has been the hardest part for me.

I nearly retched twice from the thickness of the syrup, but once it took effect, I was all in!

It's a couple of hundred dollars at a public pharmacy but only $30 at the hospital pharmacy, and I get three bottles for that price. Winner winner, chicken dinner!

I tested it with a cold latte at the hospital café, and while I couldn't taste the coffee, I also didn't have the metallic taste in my mouth, which meant I could enjoy eating.

I nearly danced down the corridor with joy! Hallelujah!

So here I go with only nine more zaps to go. Wish me luck!

UPDATE JUNE 12TH- EMBRACING THE BORING MOMENTS

❧

*M*y Original Post

*M*Y LAST WEEK *of six weeks of radiation is here!*

The last five weeks have felt like I've been in a bizarre time experiment where time went slow at times and, at others, felt reassuringly just right. What it didn't do was speed up (and how I wished it would!).

To keep perspective, I knew I needed to see my daily zaps as just another to-do in my day. Several times a week, I had to remind myself that my life did not center around radiation sessions — though, at times, it felt all-consuming.

The first week was about settling into a routine and getting into the right headspace. By far, Week 4 was my most challenging. I was angry that my four-week treatment had been extended to six. I was ready for it to end and hated the commitment of daily zaps.

The dark humor of Week 5 helped me reset and return to being in the moment. Thank you to everyone who shared your funnies with me! I love you 😊

I pledged to myself going into radiation that I would be the most boring radiation patient ever. And I've pretty much kept that commitment.

The worst thing to happen has been losing my sense of taste and everything tasting like metal. My taste sense may take up to six months to return — or it might not. We'll see!

As I said at the start, time is a funny thing. It could come back in six days, six weeks, six months, or not at all. I just need to stay in the moment I'm in and celebrate all I do have in this moment.

To date, I've had no pain. My radiation burn hasn't been itchy (except for about ten minutes last night 😁 *). I have one small sore behind my ear, but apart from that, my skin has tolerated radiation well.*

I had slight swelling in my throat during Weeks 2 to 4, but that's gone now.

My ear has taken the brunt of the zaps. It's swollen and has a small sore behind the ear lobe.

I got thrush in my mouth in Week 4, but it quickly cleared up by the end of Week 5.

I've lost a patch of hair at the back right side near my ear, which doesn't bother me because I can't see it. 😁

What I'm excited by is that my under-chin hairs on the right side have been zapped away. Sweet!

My energy levels have been pretty good. In Weeks 4 and 5, if I could nap for 2-4 hours after treatment, I was bright and sparky the rest of the time.

Everyone reacts to radiation differently, but there are inevitable reactions like radiation burns.

My radiation burns will continue to show up for up to four weeks after treatment stops, so while this week represents the end of treatment, it's not the end of side effects.

My only expectation for these six weeks was to be a boring patient, and I'm proud to be boring in this context.

Here's to my last boring radiation week!

REFLECTIONS: EMBRACING THE BORING MOMENTS

Radiation treatment is often depicted as grueling, emotional, and life-altering. And yes, there are parts of it that fit that description. But what if you make a conscious decision to be "boring" through it all?

For me, being the most boring radiation patient wasn't about denying reality — it was about managing my expectations and keeping things grounded. In a way, it became my secret superpower: staying steady, staying calm, and embracing the ordinary moments as extraordinary victories.

Because let's be honest... in life, "boring" often means uneventful. And when you're navigating something as big as cancer, no major events are a priceless gift.

Progress doesn't have to be dramatic to be meaningful. And time is a funny thing. During challenges, time can feel like it's dragging on, but it's important to stay present and find moments of joy.

KEY TAKEAWAYS FOR YOU

Here are a few things I've learned from this experience that might resonate with you:

1. Being boring can be a good thing.

Sometimes, keeping things simple and steady is the best way to get through a challenge.

2. Time is a weird construct.

Time can feel slow or fast, depending on what you're experiencing. Staying present helps you make the most of each moment.

3. Celebrate small wins.

Whether it's no pain, good energy, or zapped-away under-chin hairs, find small things to celebrate.

A PRACTICAL TAKEAWAY FOR YOU

If you're navigating a long-term challenge, try this exercise to help you stay grounded and present:

1. Set realistic expectations.

Focus on what you can control, and keep your expectations grounded.

2. Acknowledge time's weirdness.

Remind yourself that time will pass, even if it feels slow right now.

3. Find small wins to celebrate.

Look for little things that bring you joy or relief and celebrate them.

MOVING FORWARD

This chapter reminded me that staying steady and celebrating small wins can help us navigate challenging times with grace and ease.

Sometimes, being boring is the best kind of progress — because it means things are going right.

UPDATE JUNE 14TH- ALL CLEAR AND GOOD TO GO!

My Original Post

So, I got some awesome news today!

The Oncologist gave me the ALL CLEAR at our chat today!!!!

Because my surgeries were so clean, radiation was preventative, and he is happy that I am good to go on Friday.

He applauded me on how well I have tolerated radiation and for my attitude... and most excellent questions lol.

I have a post-radiation check-in in July and then 6-monthly check-ins swapping between oncology and ENT surgical to monitor.

My reaction is one of, "Of course!" lol. I guess I just always expected that I would be clear. Or maybe it simply has not hit yet!

Officially, I am cancer-free after five years, so I am taking the approach of being "all clear and good to go!"

Now for my remaining two zaps!!!

REFLECTIONS: THE POWER OF EXPECTATION AND POSITIVE MINDSET

There are certain milestones in life that mark a clear "before" and "after." Getting the "all clear" from my Oncologist was one of those moments.

I'd been through surgeries, treatments, and more zaps than I wanted to count. But when I heard those words — "all clear" — it felt like a victory lap.

What surprised me most wasn't the news itself, but my reaction. I wasn't overcome with emotion when I heard the "all clear." Instead, I felt like the outcome had already been decided in my mind. That's not to say I was naive or ignoring the seriousness of cancer — I simply believed I would be okay.

Because deep down, I had expected this outcome all along.

What I've learned through this experience is that our mindset shapes how we experience life. When you expect to be able to handle any outcomes, you carry yourself with more confidence and handle challenges with more grace.

This post also highlights the importance of ongoing monitoring and follow-ups. I'm grateful for the care team that will keep an eye on my health, and I'm committed to taking care of myself moving forward.

KEY TAKEAWAYS FOR YOU

Here are some lessons I've learned from this experience that might resonate with you:

1. Positive expectations shape your reality.

Your mindset plays a huge role in how you experience life. When you expect good outcomes, you're more likely to see opportunities and navigate challenges with confidence.

2. Milestones deserve celebration.

Hearing the "all clear" was a huge milestone for me. It's important to acknowledge and celebrate these moments in life, no matter how big or small.

3. Ongoing monitoring is essential.

Health is a continuous journey. Follow-ups and regular check-ins are crucial for maintaining well-being, even after reaching a major milestone.

A PRACTICAL TAKEAWAY FOR YOU

If you're working toward a big goal or milestone, try this exercise to help you stay positive and prepared:

1. Visualize success.

Take time to imagine the positive outcome you want. Picture yourself achieving it and how you'll feel in that moment.

2. Acknowledge your progress.

Celebrate the small wins along the way. Each step brings you closer to your goal, so take time to appreciate your journey.

3. Plan for ongoing support.

Once you reach a milestone, think about how you'll maintain progress with ongoing support or follow-ups. It's important to keep up the momentum.

MOVING FORWARD

Getting the "all clear" isn't the end of the journey — it's a new beginning.

I'm grateful for the care I've received and the support from my friends and family. Moving forward, I'm committed to staying on top of my health and continuing to nurture a positive mindset.

Because, at the end of the day, your expectations and attitude can make all the difference in how you experience life's milestones.

UPDATE JUNE 16TH - FREE AT LAST!

My Original Post

FREE! I'm free! 30 radiation sessions are done and dusted!

I'm summing up my cancer experience with these five(ish) words:

•Courage

•Resilience

•Live-in-the-present

•Mindset

•Humor

I have a-ways still to go. The effects of the radiation will continue to bake me for the next two weeks, so my burn may get worse before it gets better.

I have anywhere up to a six-month wait to see if my taste buds return and if my dry mouth will improve. Neither of these things are guaranteed to return, so I may be faced with some challenges ahead.

One day at a time, though — let's see what happens! And deal with whatever comes about.

To celebrate my last session, I bought this gorgeous shirt to wear for the first time today.

Tonight, I'm opening a present from Cheryl over FaceTime with her, and the family have a nice dinner bubbling away, and plonk chilled ready to lift a glass.

Thank you to each one of you for your support. You were there for me each step of the way, and I could not be more grateful. 🖤

REFLECTIONS: THE JOURNEY OF COMPLETION AND GRATITUDE

This post wraps up a significant chapter in my life. 30 radiation sessions complete — what a milestone!

Finishing radiation wasn't just about completing a medical treatment. It was about reaching the end of a chapter that had tested every part of me — physically, emotionally, and mentally.

My Mom was able to come to treatment with me that day and be there right at the moment I finished. This wasn't just my journey. It was one that many people had taken with me. From the friends who sent memes to make me laugh, to the family who made sure I was never alone, to the doctors and nurses who treated me with kindness and expertise — they were all part of this story.

What stands out most to me is the importance of gratitude and celebration. Even though there are still challenges ahead, it's important to acknowledge the progress and celebrate how far I've come.

The five words I chose — Courage, Resilience, Live-in-the-present, Mindset, and Humor — sum up the key lessons from this journey. They've been my guideposts, helping me navigate the toughest moments with grace and strength.

Courage

I didn't feel particularly courageous when I first heard the word "cancer." I felt scared. But courage isn't the absence of fear — it's moving forward despite the fear.

It took courage to walk into that treatment room every day, to lie down and have my mask bolted to the table, to keep showing up even when my body and mind wanted to give up.

Courage wasn't a grand gesture. It was in the small, daily acts of showing up and saying, "I'm still here."

Resilience

Resilience is one of those words that gets thrown around a lot. But living through cancer has given me a new appreciation for what it really means.

It's not about bouncing back to who you were before. It's about adapting to the new reality and finding ways to thrive in it.

Radiation changed me. My body feels different. My sense of taste is still a question mark. My energy levels fluctuate. But I've learned to adapt. To be patient. To trust that I have what it takes to navigate whatever comes next.

Live-in-the-Present

I've always been someone who plans ahead, who thinks about the future. But cancer taught me to slow down and focus on this moment.

During radiation, I couldn't think too far ahead. If I did, it became overwhelming.

So, I focused on getting through each zap. Each meal. Each day.

Living in the present isn't always easy, but it brings a sense of peace. It reminds me to appreciate what I have right now.

Mindset

If there's one thing that carried me through this journey, it's my mindset.

I've spent years working on my mindset through personal development and coaching, and it paid off in ways I never could have imagined.

When fear crept in, I had tools to calm it. When I felt overwhelmed, I had strategies to regain my balance.

Mindset isn't about being positive all the time. It's about knowing how to navigate the lows and find your way back to center.

Humor

Oh, how humor has saved me!

From the very beginning, I knew that laughter would be my lifeline. I asked my friends for dark humor, dad jokes, and silly memes — and they delivered.

Even on the hardest days, humor brought lightness. It reminded me that life is still full of joy and laughter, even in the midst of a serious health journey.

I could not stop laughing on the inside, and then outwardly once treatment was over, when the Radiation Therapists played Adele for my last treatment song. Way back in Week 1 at the start of radiation, they asked what kind of music I wanted to listen to during treatments, and I told them, "Anything except Adele — no one should be that sad and tortured!" It became a running joke over the six weeks, so when they played her on my final day, I absolutely loved their sense of humor. Well played!

This chapter reminded me that endings are new beginnings. Gratitude, courage, and humor have carried me through, and they will continue to guide me in the next chapter of life.

Gratitude for the Journey

As I look back on this chapter of my life, I feel immense gratitude.

Gratitude for the support I received. Gratitude for my body's resilience. Gratitude for the lessons I've learned.

But I'm also grateful for the tough moments — the fear, the frustration, the exhaustion.

Because those moments shaped me. They taught me what I'm capable of. They reminded me of the strength and love that surrounds me.

This isn't the end of the journey. There are still follow-ups, side effects, and uncertainties ahead. But for now, I'm celebrating this milestone.

Because today, I'm free.

Moving Forward

I've learned that life is a series of moments. Some are hard. Some are joyful. Some are downright hilarious.

What matters most is how we show up in those moments.

I'm choosing to show up with courage, resilience, presence, mindset, and humor.

And I'm choosing to live in gratitude for every step of the journey — past, present, and future.

Because, after all, I'm free.

And that's worth celebrating.

UPDATE JUNE 20TH

❧

*M*y Original Post

THIS IS my first week post-radiation, and I will admit that I am feeling a little lost.

For the last seven months, I have been a cancer patient with constraints around time and location.

The thing I wished for — the all clear — came earlier than expected (June 14th instead of July 12th), and that threw me a bit.

It is like being given the keys to the kingdom but not being able to walk through the gates into the prize.

I know my reaction is normal, but still...

On Monday, when I sat down to work, I froze.

The reason? I did not have to plan my day around radiation.

Radiation had only been for six weeks, but it had a hold on my life. You simply cannot miss a treatment, so it became a priority in my day.

I can see now I need to renew my contract with my day. What do I want to be, do, and have in my day?

I get to decide that, and I am having fun writing down ideas.

I will know when I hit the right combo.

This is my first week post-radiation, and it is a challenge from a general health perspective.

Just think of a bunch of hidden prickles in your shirt, all annoying you together and separately.

The prickles themselves are little things, but boy, do they have the power to nip at your state of being.

Last week, in the final week of radiation, the skin behind my ear broke down — think an open oozing sore.

It is gradually getting better thanks to great drugs and the expert nursing care of Kevin. 🤍

The skin on my throat is sloughing off in places.

A couple of places on my neck I thought were headed into breakdown did not, fortunately, and just remain very tender.

The skin is a mixture of burnt red, pale white, and weird brown we will not talk about.

I am not bothered by the color, but it is constantly sore and reminds me it is there whenever I turn my neck.

I continue to struggle with a cough from where the radiation has "tickled" my throat.

I like to say "tickle" rather than "burnt" to take some power away from it.

I can even snore when awake, thanks to the impact of the radiation on my throat and nose.

My taste buds remain on holidays.

My mouth continues to taste like metal, which transfers to any water and food I consume.

I have been given a pink lidocaine mixture (Mucosoothe) to swirl in my mouth 15 minutes prior to eating.

This numbs my mouth and removes the metal flavor for about 15 minutes.

It is then a rush to gobble my meal down before the metal taste comes back.

I continue to have dry mouth — think Sahara Desert dry and not "we haven't had rain for a month" dry!

The impact is that my food needs to be very moist.

REFLECTIONS: NAVIGATING LIFE AFTER RADIATION

This chapter highlights the transition period after a major life event.

I thought the end of radiation would bring immediate relief, but instead, it has brought a new set of challenges — both emotional and physical.

I have learned that healing is not linear. There are ups and downs, and it is normal to feel lost after such a structured period of time.

The concept of renewing my contract with my day stood out to me. It is about redefining my daily life now that the treatment phase is over.

KEY TAKEAWAYS FOR YOU

Here are some lessons I have learned from this experience that might help you:

1. Transitions can feel unsettling.

It is normal to feel a bit lost after a major life event ends. Give yourself grace and time to adjust.

2. Healing takes time.

Even after the "end" of a treatment, there may be lingering effects to work through. Be patient with yourself.

3. Renew your contract with your day.

Take time to redefine your daily life based on your new reality.

A PRACTICAL TAKEAWAY FOR YOU

If you are navigating a transition period, try this exercise to help you find your new rhythm:

1. Acknowledge your feelings.

It is okay to feel lost or unsure. Name those feelings and give yourself permission to sit with them.

2. Renew your contract with your day.

Write down what you want to be, do, and have in your day.

3. Focus on small adjustments.

Healing and transitions are about small steps forward. Focus on one thing at a time.

This chapter reminded me that endings are also beginnings. It is about giving yourself time to adjust and finding your new rhythm in life.

UPDATE JULY 31ST

⁂

*M*y Original Post

MY RIGHT LEG *has been swelling over the last ten days but wasn't hot or otherwise presenting as bad. I thought it was lymphoedema, which I'd been told could happen.*

I went to my doctor this morning, who ordered an ultrasound, and the results are a bit confronting.

I have a blood clot that goes from mid-calf all the way up my leg and into my stomach. It stops 3cm from the major blood vein going up. If it reaches that, it's into my lungs — and that's not good.

Now I am just waiting for the clots to dissolve. It's very weird just waiting — will it dissolve, or will it travel?!

I'm on a blood-thinning drug, Clexane (heparin), for three days, as well as Xarelto (rivaroxaban), which I'll keep taking for life now.

The pain in my upper thigh is worse than anything I've had this year. It's excruciating 😭 but this, too, shall pass.

Next steps are for me to go back to my Hematologist and get my Alive Plan sorted.

I will be on blood thinners (probably Xarelto) for life now, as this clot — and such a huge one — was spontaneous and not the result of an injury.

Apparently, my blood clotting disorder and my cancer combined are a recipe for clots.

This year is really testing my resolve lol 😅

I'm cancelling my TKR (total knee replacement) until at least 2025 (if my Orthopod will even do me then). I have a heap of healing and stabilizing to do before I can even think of that, and he may feel I'm too much at risk.

Note: I flew to Brisbane and back last week for a celebration with my dearest friend, Caroline, and the doc was amazed the clot didn't throw! I'm so grateful it didn't!!!!

I had a brief cry to Cheryl — not about the clot so much but that it would mean I couldn't fly to Norway.

Cheryl reminded me being on blood thinners is the safest thing for me. Also, there are travel insurers who will cover me, so all's good.

Norway is still on! I leave 29/2, so there's plenty of time to get well. Yippee!!!!
🐷

REFLECTIONS: NAVIGATING UNEXPECTED HEALTH CHALLENGES WITH HOPE AND PERSPECTIVE

This post highlights how life can throw curveballs when you least expect them.

I wasn't expecting to hear that I had a blood clot running from my calf to my stomach — it sounded huge, dangerous, and terrifying. The thought that it was only 3cm away from entering a major vein and potentially traveling to my lungs was enough to take my breath away.

If there is one thing I have learned from cancer is that it's important to stay focused on solutions and not let fear take over.

There still remains something unnerving about waiting. I still was not used to just sitting and letting my body do the work without any proactive steps to "fix" things. It felt like being in limbo, not knowing if the clot would dissolve or move.

But once I got past the initial fear, I realized this was another lesson in resilience. My Alive Plan — a concept I've been leaning into — reminded me that I have so much living left to do. This clot wasn't going to stop me from enjoying my life.

The hardest part wasn't the physical pain, though that was excruciating. It was the emotional hit of having to cancel my total knee replacement and the brief worry that my trip to Norway in 2024 might be in jeopardy.

Crying to Cheryl helped me process the emotions, and her reminder that blood thinners are actually keeping me safe was exactly what I needed to hear. I was back to planning my trip to Norway, excited and hopeful.

This experience also reminded me of the importance of gratitude. The fact that the clot didn't throw during my trip to Brisbane felt like a miracle. It could have gone very differently, and I'm so grateful it didn't.

Life will continue to test my resolve, but I'm still standing.

KEY TAKEAWAYS FOR YOU

Here are a few lessons I've learned from this experience that might help you:

1. Adaptability is key.

Life doesn't always go according to plan. Being adaptable can help you navigate unexpected challenges with grace and strength.

2. Focus on living.

Focusing on what you want to do and experience in life can help you push through challenges and keep your eyes on the bigger picture.

3. There's always room for hope.

Even when things feel uncertain, there's always room for joy and hope.

A PRACTICAL TAKEAWAY FOR YOU

If you're facing unexpected health challenges, try this exercise to help you stay hopeful and adaptable:

1. Create your Alive Plan.

What do you want to do, experience, and enjoy in life? Write it down and focus on it.

2. Adapt your plans as needed.

If something unexpected comes up, give yourself permission to adjust your plans while keeping your goals in sight.

3. Look for the silver linings.

Even in difficult situations, there are reasons to be hopeful. Focus on what you can still do and what brings you joy.

MOVING FORWARD

This post reminded me that unexpected health challenges don't have to stop me from living my life.

It's about adaptability, gratitude, and keeping my eyes on what's ahead — like my trip to Norway.

The Alive Plan is my reminder to keep living, keep dreaming, and keep finding joy, no matter what life throws my way.

UPDATE AUGUST 2ND-BLOOD CLOT UPDATE

*M*y Original Post

I'VE HAD QUITE *a journey with my latest health scare, and I wanted to share an update.*

I saw my Hematologist, and he's happy with the blood thinner regime I'm on. I'll continue this until I see him again in three months, at which point I'll have a new ultrasound and blood work done to reassess things.

This blood clot is one of the biggest he's seen, and we're both happy it's not bigger! Due to its size, it will take months to dissolve.

The best news ever? The doc confirmed that overseas travel is okay! Wahoo!

So, for now, it's life as usual — with some blood thinners thrown in.

Recovery Update Plus a Big Scare

I'm six weeks post-radiation, and it has passed in a flash.

My radiation burn didn't worsen after stopping treatment. In fact, within two weeks, my skin had a pink glow and was healing well.

I've lost my sense of taste, but it's starting to return. Dry mouth remains a challenge.

The Scare

Four weeks after radiation, I noticed my right ankle was swollen. I thought it was lymphoedema.

On 31 July, I was diagnosed with a 63cm blood clot from mid-calf to my stomach. It stops 3cm from the IVC, a major vein that could have taken the clot to my lungs.

If the clot had moved further, it could have been life-threatening.

My GP's treatment plan was spot on, and the Hematologist confirmed I'm on the right blood thinners.

I was scared on Monday. Far more than when I received my cancer diagnosis. The immediacy of this situation made it feel more frightening.

After a tearful chat with Cheryl, I found my balance again and got on with living my day.

In funny news, I'm walking like I just got off a horse. Wearing pants has been a challenge, and I've discovered I only own one skirt — which has gotten a lot of wear!

I'm doing good now. The pain is gradually lessening. The blood thinners are doing their job, and now it's just a matter of time.

REFLECTIONS: FACING A LIFE-THREATENING SCARE WITH RESILIENCE

When I was diagnosed with cancer, I wasn't immediately overwhelmed by fear. There was time to process and plan my next steps. But the blood clot news hit me like a freight train. The fear wasn't hypothetical; it was immediate.

The thought that something inside my body could break loose and cause life-threatening damage — without warning — was terrifying. It was different from cancer because it felt sudden, unpredictable, and entirely out of my control.

I learned that fear can sneak up on you when you least expect it. And when it does, it's okay to fall apart for a moment. I cried with Cheryl because I needed that release. It wasn't about the clot itself — it was about everything that came with it: the uncertainty, the waiting, the not knowing if I could still do the things I love.

Once I let those emotions out, I found my balance again. I reminded myself that I've already survived so much. This was just another curveball to navigate.

Gratitude played a big role in helping me shift my mindset. I was grateful the clot didn't throw during my trip to Brisbane. I was grateful for my doctor's quick action. I was grateful that I still had time to plan for Norway.

Fear is natural, but it doesn't have to define the story.

KEY TAKEAWAYS FOR YOU

1. It's okay to be scared.

Fear is a normal response to life-threatening situations. Acknowledge it, but don't let it take over.

2. Find your balance.

When you're feeling overwhelmed, find ways to reset — whether it's talking to someone you trust, journaling, or taking a walk.

3. Gratitude can shift your mindset.

Even in frightening moments, there's always something to be grateful for. Gratitude helps bring perspective and calm.

A PRACTICAL TAKEAWAY FOR YOU

If you're facing an unexpected health scare, try this exercise to help you process your emotions and find balance:

1. Name your fear.

Write down what you're afraid of. Putting it into words can help you see it more clearly.

2. Reach out to someone.

Talk to a trusted friend or family member. Sometimes, saying things out loud helps release emotional tension.

3. Make a list of three things you're grateful for.

Even in hard times, focusing on gratitude can help you regain your perspective and calm.

MOVING FORWARD

This post reminded me that life is full of surprises — some good, some not so good. But with resilience, gratitude, and a little humor, we can face anything that comes our way.

I'm grateful for the quick action of my medical team, the support of my friends and family, and the opportunity to keep living my life. Norway is still on the horizon, and I'm ready to embrace whatever comes next.

MOVING FORWARD — THE JOURNEY CONTINUES

*W*hen I look back on the past two years, I realize that this book isn't about cancer.

It's about life.

It's about the unexpected twists and turns that remind us we're stronger than we think, more resilient than we realize, and braver than we know.

Cancer was the catalyst for this particular time in my life, but the lessons I've shared aren't unique to a cancer diagnosis. We all face challenges that knock us sideways, throw us off course, and make us question how we're going to get through.

The beauty of life — and the message I want you to take from this book — is that we do get through. Not always perfectly, not always gracefully, and certainly not always without tears or fears. But we get through with humor, love, and resilience.

What This Journey Taught Me

If I had to sum up what I've learned, it's this:

- Courage isn't about not being scared. It's about showing up anyway.
- Resilience is built over time. It's the little moments of getting back up that make us strong.
- Gratitude shifts everything.
- Humor heals.

Life didn't stop after my cancer diagnosis. It didn't pause when I was told I had a blood clot that could have ended my life. Life kept going — sometimes with me crying on the floor, sometimes with me laughing my head off, sometimes with me plodding along because that was all I could do.

But through it all, I kept moving forward.

The Power of Community

One of the greatest gifts of this journey has been the community that surrounded me.

I've always been someone who gives practical support. I'd show up with a roast chicken or fold the laundry. But what I learned during my own journey is that emotional support is just as important.

The messages, the memes, the jokes, the FaceTime calls — these small acts of kindness were monumental. They reminded me that we're never truly alone, even when we feel like we are.

If there's one thing I hope this book encourages you to do, it's this: reach out. Be there for your friends, your family, your community. Not just when things are hard, but always. Because connection is the glue that holds us together.

What's Next for Me?

Am I the same person I was before this journey began? No. I'm stronger, more self-aware, and more grateful than I've ever been.

But I'm also more curious about what's next.

The journey doesn't end with the last radiation zap or the last appointment with the oncologist. Life keeps going.

I've learned that regular skin cancer checks are a must for me.

I've learned that saliva plays a crucial role in protecting teeth overnight, helping to prevent decay. With one less salivary gland, the teeth on my right side have taken a beating—meaning my dentist and I have been seeing far more of each other than I'd like!

I've learned to celebrate the small wins, cherish the people around me, and live in the moment.

I've learned to laugh at the ridiculousness of it all — because let's be honest, sneezing in a radiation mask is comedy gold. 😂

I'm still learning what life looks like with just one salivary gland. I haven't fully adapted yet, and let me tell you—summer in North Queensland, Australia, really put me to the test. The relentless dry mouth was a challenge of its own. Public speaking adds another layer, as I figure out how to work hydration into my sessions to keep my mouth from drying out mid-sentence.

I'm still learning to embrace uncertainty. In the past year, I've had two skin cancer procedures, and each time I wait for the biopsy results, I'm reminded that the best way forward is to stay present.

And I hear my Dad whispering to me, "It's all good, Narelle! You've got this!"

FOR YOU, DEAR READER

This book was written for you. Whether you're navigating your own health challenge, supporting a loved one, or simply looking for inspiration to get through a tough time, I hope my journey has resonated with you.

I want you to remember:

- You are stronger than you think.
- You are allowed to feel scared.
- You can laugh and cry at the same time.
- You are never alone.

And most importantly…

You've got this.

MOVING FORWARD TOGETHER

Life is unpredictable. It's messy. It's beautiful.

But through all its twists and turns, we keep moving forward.

Whether you're navigating the road ahead with confidence or with wobbly knees, know that you're not walking it alone.

Thank you for walking with me through this journey. Your love, laughter, and support have meant the world to me.

Cheers, Narelle

* * *

KEEP TURNING the pages as I have a number of gifts for you.

A NOTE FROM THE AUTHOR

I love a good personal development book as much as the next person, but let's be real—sometimes, the best lessons, the most soul-filling inspiration, and the biggest laugh-out-loud moments don't come from self-help books. They come from **fiction**.

Fiction has the power to transport us, to let us walk in someone else's shoes, to **see courage, resilience, and joy in action**. Whether it's a character taking on the world in their own way, a storyline that reminds us what really matters, or a heartwarming moment that lifts our spirits, stories have a way of **sneaking life lessons into our hearts without us even realizing it**.

I found this to be especially true during my own cancer journey. Some of the most practical wisdom and most-needed laughter didn't come from advice books—they came from the **characters who refused to give up, who tackled life on their own terms, and who found joy even in the hardest moments**.

If you're looking for books that **entertain while also uplifting**, I highly recommend checking out these two incredible authors:

S.E. Smith – Bold, Action-Packed, and Heartfelt

S.E. Smith is a **master of storytelling**, blending action, adventure, and romance with strong, capable heroines and the kind of heroes you'd want in your corner. Her books are full of laughter, love, and resilience—perfect when you need a story that reminds you how powerful determination and connection can be.

Recommended Reads:

📖 **Choosing Riley** – A fiercely independent woman gets kidnapped by aliens... and decides to take charge of her own fate. Full of humor and heart. Even if you are not into aliens, give this book a go because it is hilarious! You will literally be laughing out loud because it is that funny!!!

📖 **Touch of Frost** – A heartwarming romance with a **second-chance love story** set in a world where survival depends on strength and trust.

📖 **Voyage of the Defiance** – A YA sci-fi adventure full of bravery and self-discovery, proving that sometimes, you have to lose everything to find yourself.

Pauline Baird Jones – Smart, Witty, and Unforgettable

Pauline Baird Jones **writes stories with intelligence, heart, and a dash of humor**. Whether it's sci-fi adventure or romantic suspense, her books pull you in and remind you that even in the face of the impossible, resilience and love can carry you through.

Recommended Reads:

📖 **The Key** – A thrilling mix of military sci-fi, romance, and adventure as a stranded woman discovers her strength—and an unexpected ally.

📖 **Relatively Risky** – A funny, smart romantic suspense with mystery, danger, and plenty of heart.

📖 **Found Girl** – A gripping sci-fi romance with a heroine who won't be defined by her past.

Carol Van Natta – Deep, Imaginative, and Thought-Provoking

Carol Van Natta creates worlds that blend action, adventure, and romance with deep emotional connections. Her books offer escapism and inspiration, showing characters who persevere through challenges and find love in unexpected places.

Recommended Reads:

Overload Flux – A sci-fi action romance where two brilliant misfits must work together to survive and uncover a dangerous conspiracy.

Shifter Mate Magic – A paranormal romance with a tough heroine, a protective shifter, and a love that defies the odds.

And if you're looking for something visual?

TV Pick: Ted Lasso – The Ultimate Feel-Good Show

If ever there was a TV show that embodied the **themes of resilience, hope, and finding joy even in hard times**, it's *Ted Lasso*. This show is **funny, heartwarming, and full of lessons** about being true to yourself, leading with kindness, and staying in the moment. Plus, the dialogue is gold, and the characters will stay with you long after the credits roll.

Wearable Inspiration

Sometimes, the smallest reminders carry the biggest impact. During my cancer journey, I found immense reassurance in something as simple as looking down at my wrist. My bangles, each engraved with powerful messages, became my quiet cheerleaders—reminding me that no matter what was happening, It's all good.

I wore:

Live a bold life.

You are magic, own that shit.

You've got this.

Be bold. Be brave. Be badass.

Each phrase was a little spark of encouragement, helping me stay grounded and strong, especially on the tough days. Inspiration doesn't have to be big or loud; sometimes, it's just knowing you have something close to you that whispers, Keep going.

If you love the idea of wearable inspiration, check out Be Bangles. Their jewellery is a beautiful way to carry words of encouragement with you, wherever you go.

Find Inspiration Everywhere

Whatever you're going through—whether it's a health battle, a major life transition, or just a tough day—know this: **inspiration and encouragement are everywhere**. A book, a TV show, a piece of jewellery, or even a well-timed quote can be the reminder you need to keep going. It doesn't have to be a self-help book or a motivational speech—sometimes, it's fiction that gives you the courage to take the next step, a TV show that reminds you to laugh, or a bracelet that whispers, You've got this.

So seek out the things that speak to you. **Read for fun. Watch for joy. Wear words that empower you.** Let stories, big and small, remind you of your strength. Because **inspiration isn't just something you find—it's something you surround yourself with.**

Narelle

TOOLS TO LIGHT THE WAY

WORKBOOK FOR IT'S ALL GOOD... EXCEPT WHEN IT'S NOT (AND HOW TO KEEP GOING ANYWAY)

If you're ready to dive deeper into building your resilience and cultivating a powerful mindset, I've created a companion workbook for this book called, *Workbook for It's All Good... Except When It's Not (And How to Keep Going Anyway)*, to guide you every step of the way.

This step-by-step resource is designed to help you step into your strength, shed your fears, and embrace your journey with confidence.

Find it here: https://itsallgoodbook.com/workbookitsallgood

Workbook

FOR

IT'S ALL GOOD...
EXCEPT WHEN
IT'S NOT
(AND HOW TO
KEEP GOING
ANYWAY)

NARELLE TODD

* * *

WORKSHOPS

I also offer **workshops** where we dive deeper into living fully, even in the midst of uncertainty. Join me at **narelletodd.com** for upcoming events and support.

* * *

RESOURCES FOR THOSE IMPACTED BY CANCER

A cancer diagnosis changes everything in an instant. From managing treatments and appointments to navigating the emotional roller-coaster, it can feel overwhelming. I know because I've been there. That's why I created the *Living with Cancer Pack*—a set of **free** resources designed to help you stay organized, grounded, and connected to yourself throughout this journey.

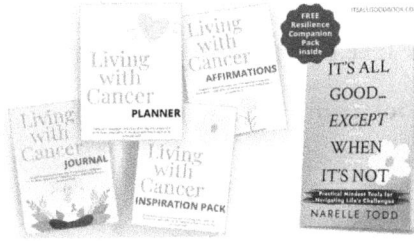

* * *

YOUR FREE *LIVING WITH CANCER* PACK

♡ **Planner** – The *Living with Cancer Planner* is your ultimate tool to keep the practicalities organized — from appointments and medications to notes and to-dos — while also encouraging you to check in with your emotional and mental well-being along the way.

♡ **Journal** – The *Living with Cancer Journal* offers you a safe space to pour out your thoughts and feelings, no matter how they show up. Whether it's a single word, a flood of emotions, or even an "I don't know what to write today," it's all part of the process. There's no right or wrong here — just your journey, one entry at a time.

♡ **Inspiration Pack** – The *Living with Cancer Inspiration Pack* features +30 thoughtfully designed posters, each carrying a message of encouragement, reflection, or motivation. These posters are perfect for adding a little light to your day, whether you display them on your mirror, pin them to a vision board, or choose one as a focus for your meditation or reflection.

♡ **Affirmations** – The *Living with Cancer Affirmations* are your companions for every kind of day. Whether you're celebrating progress, bracing for a tough moment, or simply needing a reminder of your strength, these affirmations are here to lift you up and keep you grounded.

Think of these as your sidekicks for the journey ahead.

🔗 **Download your free Living with Cancer Pack here:**

https://itsallgoodbook.com/livingwithcancerpack

✳ ✳ ✳

PEACE & POWER PLAYBOOK

The *Peace & Power Playbook* is a guided workbook designed to help you find your center and navigate cancer on *your* terms. The world has plenty of opinions about what you should do, how you should feel, and what healing should look like — but your voice is the one that matters. In this playbook, I walk you through a series of simple but powerful exercises to help you regain clarity, build inner strength, and move forward with confidence. Because peace and power aren't about fighting harder; they're about standing firm in *your* truth.

🔗 **Get your free copy here:**

https://itsallgoodbook.com/peacepowerplaybook.

✳ ✳ ✳

You're not alone in this. These resources are here to support you, so you can move through each day with clarity, strength, and self-compassion.

Because even when life gets tricky, you've got this... and a little extra support never hurts. It's all good!

Cheers, Narelle 🤍

ABOUT THE AUTHOR

Narelle Todd is a self-described coffee enthusiast, marketing maverick, and mindset mentor who has spent the last 30 years coaching individuals to live their best lives—personally, professionally, and creatively. As the founder of GetMyBookOutThere.com and NarelleTodd.com, she has helped self-published fiction authors turn their invisible stories into reader-favorite autobuys, selling millions of ebooks along the way. Combining her passion for mindset coaching with her business savvy, Narelle is also a life coach who empowers women to navigate life's transitions with resilience, calm, and joy.

Armed with a Master of Education (Training and Development) and Graduate Management qualifications, Narelle brings a unique blend of academic knowledge and real-world experience to her work. With three decades of coaching and HR expertise, she's a pro at simplifying complex challenges into elegant, actionable solutions tailored to her clients' unique needs. Her lighthearted, practical, and results-driven approach inspires trust and action.

When Narelle isn't coaching or helping authors build thriving businesses, she's likely jet-setting to her next adventure, sipping iced coffee in the tropics, or braving the icy winds of her favorite cold-weather getaways. Known for her quirky sense of humor, love of growth (both personal and in her garden), and her commitment to living authentically, Narelle is living proof that success doesn't have to come at the cost of joy.

Ready to take your mindset, business, or book sales to the next level? Visit Narelle at NarelleTodd.com and start your journey today!

Cheers!